CultureShock!
A Survival Guide to Customs and Etiquette

Sri Lanka

Robert Barlas
Nanda P Wanasundera

Marshall Cavendish
Editions

This 5th edition published in 2009 by:
Marshall Cavendish Corporation
99 White Plains Road
Tarrytown NY 10591-9001
www.marshallcavendish.us

First published in 1996 by Times Editions Pte Ltd, reprinted 1996, 1997, 1998, 1999; 2nd edition published in 2000, reprinted 2000; 3rd edition published in 2003, reprinted 2003; 4th edition published in 2006.
© 2009 Marshall Cavendish International (Asia) Private Limited

Other Marshall Cavendish Offices:
Marshall Cavendish International (Asia) Pte Ltd. 1 New Industrial Road, Singapore 536196 ■ Marshall Cavendish Ltd. 5th Floor, 32-38 Saffron Hill, London EC1N 8FH, UK ■ Marshall Cavendish International (Thailand) Co Ltd. 253 Asoke, 12th Flr, Sukhumvit 21 Road, Klongtoey Nua, Wattana, Bangkok 10110, Thailand ■ Marshall Cavendish (Malaysia) Sdn Bhd, Times Subang, Lot 46, Subang Hi-Tech Industrial Park, Batu Tiga, 40000 Shah Alam, Selangor Darul Ehsan, Malaysia

Marshall Cavendish is a trademark of Times Publishing Limited

ISBN: 978-07614-5678-0

Please contact the publisher for the Library of Congress catalogue number

Printed in Singapore by Times Printers Pte Ltd

Photo Credits:
All black and white photos from Robert Barlas, Priyanjan Suresh de Silva and Rajiv Wanasundera except page vii (Photolibrary). All colour images from Photolibrary except pages l–m (Lonely Planet Images). ■ Cover photo: Photolibrary

All illustrations by TRIGG

ABOUT THE SERIES

Culture shock is a state of disorientation that can come over anyone who has been thrust into unknown surroundings, away from one's comfort zone. *CultureShock!* is a series of trusted and reputed guides which has, for decades, been helping expatriates and long-term visitors to cushion the impact of culture shock whenever they move to a new country.

Written by people who have lived in the country and experienced culture shock themselves, the authors share all the information necessary for anyone to cope with these feelings of disorientation more effectively. The guides are written in a style that is easy to read and covers a range of topics that will arm readers with enough advice, hints and tips to make their lives as normal as possible again.

Each book is structured in the same manner. It begins with the first impressions that visitors will have of that city or country. To understand a culture, one must first understand the people—where they came from, who they are, the values and traditions they live by, as well as their customs and etiquette. This is covered in the first half of the book.

Then on with the practical aspects—how to settle in with the greatest of ease. Authors walk readers through topics such as how to find accommodation, get the utilities and telecommunications up and running, enrol the children in school and keep in the pink of health. But that's not all. Once the essentials are out of the way, venture out and try the food, enjoy more of the culture and travel to other areas. Then be immersed in the language of the country before discovering more about the business side of things.

To round off, snippets of basic information are offered before readers are 'tested' on customs and etiquette of the country. Useful words and phrases, a comprehensive resource guide and list of books for further research are also included for easy reference.

CONTENTS

FOREWORD

Culture in ancient times was defined as 'the sum total of the equipment of the human individual which enables him to be attuned to his immediate environment on the one hand and to the historical past on the other'. It reflects, in effect, what humans have added to nature. It comprises the spiritual, material, intellectual and emotional features of a society and includes, in addition to the arts and letters, the value systems, traditions, modes of life and beliefs of that society. It also absorbs from other cultures and undergoes changes with time, sometimes beneficial, sometimes regressive.

The Sri Lankan culture, an ancient one steeped in tradition yet influenced by its linguistic, ethnic and religious diversity, as well as by its historical past, is no exception. To a foreigner visiting the country, whether for a short or a long stay, the visual and other manifestations of this culture could be fascinating, depending largely on his attitude and knowledge and his acceptance of the dignity and value of every culture as part of the common heritage of mankind.

Robert Barlas and Nanda Wanasundera have first-hand knowledge of the problems faced by foreign guests in our country when they try to adjust to living in a cultural environment different from their own. They have written this very readable and informative book as a guide to those who will visit our shores and share our culture with us.

Earle Samarasinghe
Former co-ordinator of Technical Assistance
to Asia and the Pacific Bureau for
Development Co-operation, UNESCO, Paris

Be welcomed by the warm hospitality of the Sri Lankans.

ACKNOWLEDGEMENTS

The most important contributors to this book have been the people of Sri Lanka themselves. Wherever I have travelled, there has always been someone who was willing and able to explain, arrange or just to lend a hand when one was wanted. By far my biggest debt of gratitude in this respect is, of course, to my co-author, Nanda Wanasundera, without whom this book would not exist in the form that it does. Nanda's encyclopaedic knowledge of the country, its people and their customs made writing the book so much easier and ensured that the 'foreign' author had his feet firmly rooted in reality.

Of course, there are also other people without whose help the writing of this book would have been impossible. Foremost among these is Babsi Direckse, my driver and friend on a number of trips around Sri Lanka, whose intimate knowledge of the country and its roads led us to some very interesting places! K G L Chandrasena was of immense assistance in guiding us to good sources of illustrations, particularly to the artist Tharaswin and the photographer Suresh de Silva, while Chitra Siriwardene and Rajadurai Surenthiran, my colleagues, helped me by explaining many puzzling nuances of the Sinhala and Tamil languages. Rajiv Wanasundera supplied most of the photographs, so also the meticulously drawn map of Sri Lanka indicating in miniature style what a town or place is famous for. Mike Noak and Mary Warnhammar were another pair of expatriate eyes and proofread the text, while Shrianjani de Alwis did the same job from the local perspective. My secretary, Ann Karunaratne, spent much time typing and refining the text without complaint. Last, but by no means least, my wife Nancy, who spent many long hours making tea and suggestions—most of which were constructive! I owe a great debt of thanks to her.

Robert Barlas

Sincere thanks to Bob Barlas for inviting me to collaborate on this book. I have spent many happy hours talking with him about my much loved country and its people. I also want to thank my sons Dharshan and Rajiv, and my husband Suriya for advice and support; and Rajiv for his photographs and outlined map.

Nanda Wanasundera

MAP OF SRI LANKA

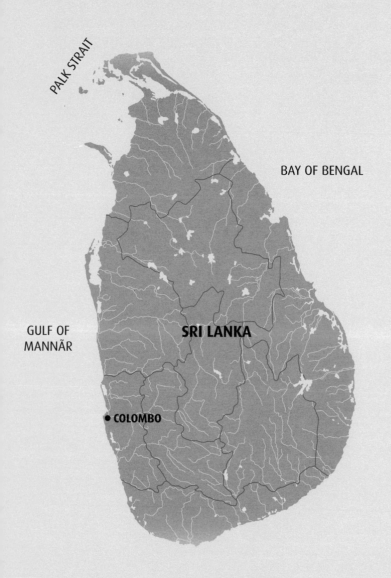

PALK STRAIT

BAY OF BENGAL

GULF OF
MANNÃR

SRI LANKA

● **COLOMBO**

INDIAN OCEAN

FIRST IMPRESSIONS

CHAPTER 1

'Read therefore the Book itself,
and you will find your self taken Captive indeed...'
—Robert Knox in the preface to
An Historical Relation of Ceylon

HEAT AND HUMIDITY FIRST WHACK THE VISITOR to Sri Lanka as s/he emerges from the newly refurbished Bandaranaike International Airport at Katunayaka, roughly 30 km north of Colombo. To compensate for this initial shock, the visitor meets smiling Sri Lankan faces. A second shock awaits the visitor: the drive to Colombo, where driving seems to be suicidal and one fears for one's safety. But like all else, there is method in the mayhem. When the visitor is able to take his eyes off the road, he sees life spilling on it with wayside vendors and small businesses selling their wares from pharmaceuticals to pottery to fruits, including the *tambili* (yellow young coconuts) which the visitor will soon come to know as a superior substitute for bubbly bottled drinks.

There's smiles all around and friendliness prompting constant overtures for embarking on conversation with the preliminary, "From where are you? Do you like it in Sri Lanka? Is it too hot?" This could be annoying and had better be nipped in the bud if the visitor gets the gut feeling the conversationalist is being intrusive and promises to be a nuisance. The pleader for a tip, the conman, the pimp and the tout are other undesirables that may be met at the airport exit itself and spreading out. Firm rudeness is called for here. But if one is in a suitable place where a conversation can be started with a sincere local, then go ahead. Many a helping hand and a friendship have been extended and forged this way. Except the streetwise, and of course the beggars, the other strangers one meets as one walks around or travels in a bus or train are usually dignified, decent and trustworthy. In rural Sri Lanka, especially in the hill country and the north central areas, the typical Sri Lankan villager is as yet a person of solid values and integrity.

An irritation soon met with is the disorderly queue, the unformed line before most counters in some banks, post offices and retail outlets. The best defensive tactic is to insist on your place in the queue; demand space between you and your hard-breathing hehind-standee and keep your cool. Avoid educating those present on proper queue forming; it's water off a duck's back! The foreigner who has come to Sri Lanka to work and live in the country often gets annoyed at being labelled a tourist, and may be at a disadvantage when visiting cultural sites particularly. Apart from these annoyances, one will meet with respect; not only respect as a person but respect for one's space and privacy.

Robert Knox

The quotation at the start of this chapter and of each subsequent chapter in this book is from Robert Knox's eye-witness account of Sri Lanka, *An Historical Relation of Ceylon*, which he wrote during his enforced stay in this country and was published on his escape and return to England in 1681.

Knox was an English sailor who was taken captive by the King of Kandy in 1659 while on a trading mission to the east coast of Sri Lanka for the East India Company. He was kept under house arrest in a village—Eladatta—close to Kandy. His observations of the country during the 20 years of captivity are the first written about the country in English, and still in many ways the best and most perceptive. The book is delightful reading, even today, not only for its detailed and precise descriptions of everything pertaining to the King of Kandy and the people of Ceylon, but also as a travelogue. Knox's style is superb: wittily tongue-in-cheek, but at the same time striving to give a factual account of the Kandyan Kingdom in the 17th century.

A complaint is that people of the country are generally not well informed; say in giving directions to a traveller. But this need be no bother since maps are freely available and sign posting is in the three languages, now more in English. Also, almost everyone has at least a basic knowledge of English.

In the workplace, unless it's a private institution/organisation, there is most definitely an air of 'taking it easy'. This laid-back ambience is most noticeable in public offices where workers chat with each other while they attend to their work; or worse, read newspapers at their desks; or worst, are busy enjoying their several cups of tea. Aggravating this situation is the number of public holidays Sri Lankans enjoy: two per major religion (8–10 days), and others celebrating new years, workers' day and independence. Every month, the full moon day is a holiday—Poya—first given as a placating concession to the majority religion. Newly arrived expatriates may be caught off guard by the Poya holidays which are 'dry' and meatless days. These all add up to around 30 days.

In most establishments, apart from shops, the working week is five days. Except for the supermarkets and some outlets, most shops open at 10:00 am in the morning and close by 6:30 pm. This often means that employers have to grant short leave to their employees who need to 'go shopping for a special occasion'. The number of days allocated as paid leave is also generous.

The food, of course—typical Sri Lankan food—is a shock to the system and introduction to it needs care and caution. It is not only the fiery chilli that bothers the foreign palate used to blander food, but also the spices generously added to curry, one of which is a mixture of condiments carrying the name *thunapaha*, which translated reads three-five! But if you get used to Sri Lankan curry, it could be an experience. A typical Sri Lankan rice and curry meal is a very nutritious meal with cooked, fried and raw dishes, with the ever present onion sambal. The variety of fruits, their variant textures and tastes, are a continuing, very pleasant surprise to the expatriate.

Men seem to be the bosses in the home and elsewhere, but once discernment is honed, it becomes evident that the country is matriarchal. There is equality among the sexes; women are emancipated even among conservative Muslims and traditional Hindus. Women seem to be taking over the breadwinning role, even though not the single parent. Men, especially at the lower rungs of

The general Sri Lankan is a political creature with voting at elections invariably in the above 80 per cent range. But politics and everything else gives way to cricket; the entire nation almost coming to a standstill when the Sri Lankan team fights a crucial match. Sri Lanka, like India and Pakistan, is truly cricket crazy!

employment, appear to depend more and more on mothers, sisters and wives.

Globalisation has taken over, Sri Lanka being the first in the sub-region to open its economy to market forces in 1977. One evidence is that most women reserve the traditional *sari* for only very formal occasions and wear western style clothes to office and elsewhere.

First impressions prove that the country is a Third World nation, still developing and slowly. But once you get closer to the real Sri Lanka, the gracious Sri Lanka, the cultured Sri Lanka, you get the distinct feeling that a stay in the country will be an experience—a happy, enriching experience. It is not for nothing that the word serendipity was coined by Horace Walpole in 1754 because of 'the faculty of making happy chance finds' in this island, formerly known as Serendip.

OVERVIEW OF THE LAND AND HISTORY

CHAPTER 2

'How this island lyes with respect into the
Neighbouring Countries, I shall not speak at all...
my design being to relate such things only that are
new and unknown unto these European Nations.'
—Robert Knox

THE LAND OF POTENTIAL

One of the strongest impressions that any visitor to Sri Lanka gets very quickly is of the enormous—and largely untapped—potential of the place. The country is bursting with opportunities that have been frustrated for so many years that now they seem almost unachievable, though achingly obvious.

At the coming of independence in 1948 from British rule, many observers of Asia felt that Sri Lanka, with its relatively small size, well-developed infrastructure, intelligent people and a high literacy rate—way above those of the other countries in the sub-region—would be the country to lead the newly emerging Asian nations into the second half of the 20th century. This has unfortunately not proved to be the case, as Sri Lanka's troubled political climate has continually retarded her progress, and she is nowhere near most of the South-east Asian countries nor India. Until such time as the problems which still bedevil the country can be satisfactorily resolved, it is very unlikely that much long-term real development will take place.

Of these problems, the most troublous has been the 26-year civil war waged by a Tamil terrorist group, the Liberation Tigers of Tamil Eelam (LTTE), demanding a separate state for the Tamils, notwithstanding the fact that Tamils lived and live peacefully all across the island. Sri Lankan Tamils (to distinguish them from the Indian-descended Tamils who live and work in the plantations of central Sri Lanka) were concentrated in the North—the Jaffna Peninsula—where the Tigers first did battle. They are in equal numbers to the Sinhalese and Muslims in the Eastern Province. Defeated during the different phases of the war, the Tigers consolidated themselves in the Wanni, just below the Jaffna Peninsula and in pockets in the east of the Island. They set up a de facto government in the Wanni with Kilinochchi as their capital. Starting in July 2006, the civil war escalated and soon the government forces defeated the Tigers in the east. Their leaders, disillusioned with the Tiger Supremo, Velupillai Prabhakaran and his megalomaniac autocracy, had offered to cooperate with the government since 2004. The Eastern Province had its provincial council elections in 2008 and the former Tiger fighter, S Chandrakanthan, is Chief Minister, while his commanding officer Vinayagamoorthi Muralitharan (aka as Karuna) is a Minister of State in the central government.

At the time of writing, the war in the Vanni is very nearly over; Parbhakaran defeated and Sri Lanka unified under the legitimately elected government with Mahinda Rajapakse as President.

The tourist industry is perhaps the clearest example of this presence of potential but unfortunate obstacles in the path of progress. In the late 1970s, it was correctly presumed that Sri Lanka had tremendous promise as an Indian Ocean cultural and beach paradise, particularly for European travellers grown weary of the Mediterranean beaches. Vast sums of money were poured into hotels, tour companies and tourist services, and for a while, it looked as though the concept would mushroom and become a tremendous foreign currency asset for Sri Lanka. After the racial riots in 1983, the tourist industry collapsed, and in spite of periodic attempts to revive it—usually destroyed by foreign news reports of disturbances in the country—tourism did not recover fast enough. With the brokered peace between the government and the LTTE, the number of tourists arriving for sea, sun and sand of the coastal areas and culture and eco-tourism increased. The tsunami of 26 December 2004 destroyed much of the coastal areas and many tourist hotels. Reconstruction and rehabilitation are complete. Like the proverbial phoenix rising from the ashes, better infrastructure improved the devastated areas. Though tourism picked up, it was again badly affected by the escalation of the war in the north and suicide bombers detonating buildings and targeting people elsewhere. The east coast is a holiday makers paradise and is fast being completely freed of the LTTE-in-hiding and sporadic killings, mostly of innocent villagers.

Tourism however never died down completely. There are always visitors to the Island, the European visitor outnumbered by the Asian—the Japanese, Chinese, and Indian.West Asians too come over for comparatively cheap stays in expensive multi-starred hotels.

A BRIEF TOUR OF SRI LANKAN HISTORY

If we wish to understand what makes modern Sri Lanka tick, a small dip into history explains a lot. Like any country, but perhaps especially Sri Lanka, the happenings of the past have conditioned the present, and so knowing something about the Sri Lankan background is almost a necessity for those who want a more intimate knowledge of the country and its people.

The development of Sri Lanka from its ancient origins to the modern day is a story of constant—and in many ways repetitive—struggle. The in-fighting for political control continues today. The desire by foreign powers to possess for themselves the richness of Sri Lanka's geographic position and its natural resources has its roots in ancient wars and grievances which have continued in one form or another for the last 25 centuries!

Until the 5th century BC, Sri Lanka (called Ceylon before 1972) was the domain of various tribes. Some time in the 5th century BC, the first of what were to become many invasions into Sri Lanka from India took place. This one was by the legendary founder of modern Sri Lanka, Prince Vijaya from Bengal. Banished from his country by his father for profligacy, Vijaya, legend says, arrived in north-east Sri Lanka in 483 BC. By his marriage to Queen Kuveni, he was invited to rule the part of the land that was hers. Vijaya wanted to start a real, royal dynasty, although he had a son and daughter by Kuveni, so banishing them, he brought over a princess from India. They were childless but his brother had children, and so the Vijaya clan were the progenitors of the Sinhala race, he being from the Singha clan in Bengal. Kuveni's children begat children who by legend became the Veddhas of Ceylon, whose tribe still exists in villages around Mahiyangana to the east of the central hills.

Vijaya's arrival is not the most important event of early Sri Lankan history. What eclipsed it was the arrival of Buddhism in Sri Lanka in about 250 BC, brought to the island by Mahinda Thera, son of the powerful Indian ruler, Emperor Asoka, who had himself been converted to Buddhism. This was during the reign of Devanampiyatissa (307–267 BC). The new religion quickly became—and still remains—the country's major religion. Buddhism also instigated a spurt forwards in culture with stupas being constructed, stone sculptor surpassing those of even India, and the Dhamma (teachings of the Buddha) being committed to writing for the first time in Aluvihara, Matale in Central Sri Lanka. Buddhism too had its ups and downs, cruelly suppressed by the Portuguese invaders but openly practiced thereafter, during colonial times.

Time passed, successive generations of South Indian kings cast greedy eyes on Sri Lanka and its rich natural resources and sporadic waves of invasions were mounted to wrest control of these riches from the original settlers with their newly acquired national identity. Under pressure from these attacks, the Sinhalese moved their capital city successively from its first location at Anuradhapura to Polonnaruwa and then briefly to Dambadeniya, Kurunegala and then to Gampola, each city further to the south than its predecessor and closer to the west coast, which was to become the focal point of Sri Lanka in later history. By 1400, the capital had reached the west coast city of Kotte where the fort of Jayawardenapura was built to serve as the Sinhalese administrative centre.

By 1505, the island of Sri Lanka was home to three distinct kingdoms. The king in Kotte controlled only the western part of the island, while the king of Jaffna was in firm control of the north. In the central mountains, previously considered only important as a refuge for those who needed a temporary hiding place, there was rapidly developing a new and vigorous splinter kingdom based in the city of Kandy, intent on establishing its own independence.

Then the Portuguese arrived. They were after cinnamon—the major product of the so-called 'spice isles'—and they wanted a monopoly in the trade. At first, they were not really interested in territorial gains, as these would have required large infrastructure to support them, but merely in making sure that what value Sri Lanka had to the outside world was theirs to exploit. However, evidence of permanent Portuguese settlement soon became obvious; forts, houses and churches began to spring up all along the west coast of the island, especially with the building of large fortified ports in maritime cities in the 1570s. Gradually, by accident rather than design, and mainly through either making alliances with local kings or simply killing them in battle, the Portuguese became the *de facto* rulers of the entire island—with the notable exception of the kingdom of Kandy—and the island of Sri Lanka became, to all intents and purposes, a Portuguese colony. These first European invaders introduced Roman Catholism to Sri Lanka and soon enough attempted mass conversion along with cruel suppression of the two major religions followed in the land: Buddhism and Hinduism.

However, the Dutch, whose power elsewhere in Asia was steadily increasing at this time, were already casting envious eyes over the lucrative Portuguese cinnamon trade, and an invitation from the King of Kandy to help him drive the Portuguese out of the island was eagerly accepted in a treaty signed in 1638. The Kandyan kingdom, with whom they were still nominally allied, soon become the only native monarchy in Sri Lanka, and, as the Kandyans themselves soon found out, the Dutch had no intention of allowing it to remain there for long either! Unlike the Portuguese, the Dutch were not unwilling colonisers, so the original treaty under which the Dutch had helped the Kandyans drive out the Portuguese was soon abrogated, and the period of Dutch colonisation in Sri Lanka rapidly developed into a battle between the Kandyan kingdom, whose influence extended into the cinnamon growing areas in the lowlands, and the Dutch settlers who controlled the export of the spice from the coastal ports. The Dutch bequeathed to the land a network of boat-navigable canals, the Dutch Reformed Church and Roman Dutch Law.

Many maritime forts like the one in Galle are testimony of their occupation of the Island.

Then came the British in 1796, who, unlike the Portuguese and the Dutch, were not only interested in the control of what natural resources were already in the island and their trading monopolies, but also in creating and trading in their own products, using the fertile soil of the island to grow them. Methodically and deliberately, they drove the Dutch from the island and then in turn defeated the last bastion of Sinhalese power in the Kandyan kingdom, not so much through strategic prowess and superior arms they had but through disunity and treason by courtiers of the Kandyan Kingdom. The last King of Kandy, Sri Wickreme Rajasinghe (1798–1815) and his beautiful wife were banished to South India. The king died in exile in 1832. The Kandyan Convention was signed in 1815, handing full power over the last kingdom of resistance to foreign invasion and domination. Sri Lanka was thus a full fledged colony of the British Empire, governed by a British Governor and administered from the tip of the northern peninsula to Dondra Head in the South by members of the British Civil Service.

The British began the active encouragement of British settlers throughout the island, and plantations soon sprang upall over the place—at first cinnamon, coconut and coffee. For the first time in a long while, the whole of Sri Lanka settled down as one nation, even if under an alien power, and suffering the consequences of being a subject race. In the 1870s, a disastrous leaf disease all but eliminated the coffee bushes throughout the island, and tea soon began to replace coffee as the island's staple plantation crop, which it remains to this day, along with coconut and rubber as secondary cash crops.

One major negative of the tea industry was the import of labour from South India to work on the tea estates, since the Sinhalese, through pride probably, refused to work on the land that had been grabbed from them by the white rulers. These Tamils of Indian origin were stateless until a pact between Sirimavo R Bandaranaike, the world's first woman prime minister and the Indian prime minister, Lal Bahadur Shastri, was signed in the 1960s sending back some of the redundant Indian labour to India and conferring Sri Lankan citizenship on the rest.

Independence from the British Raj eventually came peacefully to Sri Lanka on 4 February 1948, as a side effect as it were, of independence granted to India after many years of bitter struggle and thousands left dead in the subcontinent, in spite of Mahatma Gandhi's policy of non-violence. The legacy of the British to Sri Lanka was considerable, almost adequately balancing the negatives of colonialism and the exploitation of local labour and lands for growing of cash crops, profits of which went to Britain.

The British left behind good infrastructure, having built roads and railway lines criss-crossing the land to enable them to rule their acquired territory and to transport their tea to Colombo from the central hill country. They also gave the land the English language, education with the starting of missionary schools in cities big and small, Anglican and other branches of the Christian religion, English law, efficient British civil servants and a system of government based on their Westminster style.

Sri Lanka's first prime minister, D S Senanayake, affectionately called the 'Father of the Nation' spent more effort on the rehabilitation of the Sri Lankan peasant, particularly the Kandyan peasant, who had been displaced from his lands and marginalised by the tea planting white entrepreneur. He encouraged subsistence farming and opened up colonisation schemes in the Dry Zone which had been all but abandoned due to the onslaught of malaria. The outlook for the future appeared good: all the racial groups had accepted the terms of independence and were represented in the new parliament,

The Independence Commemoration Hall in Colombo 7, built in the 1950s.
Queen Elizabeth ceremonially opened a session of parliament here
The 'Father of the Nation', D S Senanayake, stands in the foreground,
immortalised in bronze.

particularly the large Tamil—and potentially troublesome—minority in the north.

The seeds of division surfaced once the restraining hand of the British was removed. In 1956, The Official Language Act (the Sinhala-only Bill) quickly gave Sinhala speakers an advantage they had not had before and reduced those who did not speak Sinhala to second-class citizenship status. No one group did this infuriate more than the Tamils, who had, under the British, secured top jobs due to their fluency in the English language and readiness to work hard and obey. The British did follow a policy of 'divide and rule' in Ceylon too; not so obvious or outrageous as their causing friction between the Hindu and Muslim populations in India. But it is a fact that when local personnel were selected for administrative jobs, the Tamils were first choice. Also they were better qualified, Jaffna having a concentration of large schools founded and funded by American missionaries. Sri Lanka was rapidly split into two warring factions: the Sinhalese majority in the south and west and the Tamil minority, whose influence in the north and east of the country had always been considerable. As the insistence on the use of Sinhala grew (even substituting a Sinhala letter for an English one on car licence plates, which led to rioting), under the then prime minister, S W R D Bandaranaike, the Tamils grew more alienated from the government and demands for their own autonomous homeland in the north began to be heard. Tamil political groups emerged, among them the LTTE, whose Tamil Tigers advocated the use

Bandaranaike Memorial International Conference Hall, a gift of the Chinese in memory of S W R D Bandaranaike, who gave the 'common man' a place in the sun. His widow, Sirimavo, was the world's first female prime minister.

of violence to gain their objective of independence from the Sinhalese majority. They were a terrorist outfit which waged guerrilla war, and was soon recognised as the most committed and most violent of terrorists, introducing to the world at large suicide bombers—men and women taped with explosives who blew up persons and buildings and themselves.

A new political force, the JVP (Janatha Vimukthi Peramuna), an extreme leftwing organisation made up of frustrated and largely educated, unemployed youth, soon came on the scene in south Sri Lanka, and serious rioting broke out in 1971, the aim of the group being to destabilise the government of Sirimavo R Bandaranaike. The uprising was suppressed by the government, but the seeds of discontent were by now formally in place. In addition was the opposition of the Tamils in the north to any form of Sinhalese nationalism, and the gradual emergence of the LTTE claiming to be the single voice of the Tamils, but soon deteriorating to a vicious terrorist group. They demanded the entire north and east as their homeland—one-third the land area and more than half the coast of Sri Lanka for around 12 per cent of the population. Conflict soon escalated to a full blown war and just as the government forces were poised to vanquish the LTTE forces, India stepped in.

J R Jayawardhena, the then president of Sri Lanka and Rajiv Gandhi, then prime minister of India, signed an agreement calling for peace. The constitution was amended in 1986 to include the provision of devolution of power to the provinces in a bid to satisfy the LTTE and Tamil aspirations for greater autonomy.

The advent of the Indian army in Sri Lanka in a peace-keeping role in 1987 only marginally helped the situation, as, although the violence of the LTTE was curtailed, serious resentment surfaced throughout the country at having 'an army of occupation' from a foreign power stationed on its soil. The JVP reared its aggressive head again and brought much destruction and repression to Central and South Sri Lanka. Its fear mongering and destabilising activities were curtailed and crushed at the very end of 1989, when its leader, Rohana Wijeweera, was arrested along with others, taken to a JVP safe house and killed in an ensuing gun battle.

Peace came to Sri Lanka; later the JVP emerged as a party in mainstream politics and life was back to normal in all of the island except for the Jaffna and Batticaloa areas.

The government sent away the peace-keeping Indian force in March 1990. Negotiations between the government and the LTTE were under way for a permanent and peaceful solution when the LTTE suddenly attacked police stations and army camps in the north and east. A large number were displaced due to the ethnic cleansing of Sinhala and Muslim peoples from Tiger held and adjoining areas. The Central Bank in Colombo and the Katunayake International Airport were attacked by LTTE suicide bombers. The LTTE also shot at pilgrims in the holiest of holy places in Anuradhapura—the sacred Bo Tree, and bombed the Temple of the Tooth in Kandy. The government with Chandrika B Kumaratunge as prime minister, which came to power in August 1994, attempted a negotiated peace with devolution of power. Both were rejected by the LTTE. When she sought election as president in 1996, she was attacked by a LTTE suicide bomber at a political meeting. She survived with her life but lost an eye. Several leaders including President Premadasa were assassinated by the LTTE.

In 2001, with the formation of a United National Party government with Ranil Wickremasinghe as prime minister, a peace agreement with LTTE Supremo, Velupillai Prabhakaran, was signed, facilitated by the Norwegian government. Security checks on roads and buildings were removed; the A9 highway connecting Colombo with Jaffna re-opened and peace prevailed, however tenuous.

Personal Safety in Sri Lanka

When any foreigner plans to come to Sri Lanka—especially for an extended stay—concern about personal safety is always an issue in making a decision. What is important to understand about Sri Lanka, however, is that the conflict that exists is purely an internal one, in which foreigners are not involved and are not an issue. In spite of the constant reports of violence in the world media, very little of it is evident to the foreigner as he goes about his daily business and only very rarely does it impinge upon his routine. Living in and/or visiting Sri Lanka is as safe, on the whole, as in any other country, and a foreigner coming to 'the Paradise Isle' need be prepared to take no greater precautions for his own personal safety than he would—out of ordinary common sense—in any other Asian country.

In the presidential election of 2005 November, the LTTE rewarded Ranil Wickremasinghe with no votes from Jaffna and all LTTE controlled or influenced areas. Tamils were prevented from voting; the majority of votes would have gone to Mr Wickremasinghe, since he was the favoured candidate by the minorities. Consequently, Mahinda Rajapakse, a Sri Lanka Freedom Party candidate who forged a coalition with the JVP and a newly formed party of Buddhist monks, calling themselves the Jatika Hela Urumaya (JHU), won the presidential election. President Rajapakse followed his predecessors in a conciliatory, non-combative approach to the Tigers, facilitated by the Peace Monitors headed by Norway and Japan. Peace talks were proposed, but the LTTE backed out more than once at the eleventh hour.

During the period of the negotiated peace, the LTTE could move around freely. Their leaders made several trips to European states and Norway particularly, while government armed forces were confined to their barracks. It was suspected, and later confirmed, that the LTTE had rebuilt its armed forces and Black Tiger navy. Large containers of goods were sent to the Vanni without any examination or restriction.

The LTTE was totally in command of the Vanni with its a de facto Tiger government, overseeing the eastern territory stretching south from Trincomalee to far below Batticaloe.

On 26 July 2006, the LTTE closed the sluice gates at Mavil Auru in the eastern hinterland which supplied water to 15,000 villages occupied by Sinhalese, Muslim and Tamils. The resident Monitoring Mission led by Norway used all their persuasive powers to have the Tamils reopen the sluice, which delivered water not only for irrigation but even for drinking and household needs. The LTTE did not budge. President Rajapakse had no alternative but to call out the Sri Lanka air force and the army to dislodge the obstructing Tiger cadres. They did this and thus started Eelam War IV.

Both the army commander—Lt. General Sarath Fonseka, and the presidential advisor on state security—Gotabhaya Rajapakse, narrowly escaped LTTE suicidal attempts on their lives. Sarath Fonseka had a suicide bomber, in the guise of a pregnant woman, throwing herself at his car within the army headquarters premises. He was seriously injured but was soon at the helm of the reinforced attack on the terrorists.

Eelam IV saw the most ferocious fighting in all the 26 years of the civil war. The LTTE launched air attacks successfully on the air force base at Anuradhapura and an oil installation facility on the outskirts of Colombo. Their commander was Prabhakaran's son, who majored in aeronautics in a university in Britain. The three light planes however were downed when they attempted to wreak havoc from the air in Colombo and Katunayake in February 2009.

The civil war is over and Prabhakaran has been defeated at the time of writing this revision. The two-and-a-half decade civil war that attempted to carve out a Tamil nation in the tiny Island of Sri Lanka had caused the death of more than 70,000 people including armed forces personnel, LTTE cadres and civilians butchered by the LTTE in their frequent marauding raids. This is the official figure; the real could be much higher. Thousands have been injured and permanently incapacitated. Tens of thousands have been displaced. The worst of the war was the last stand of the LTTE Supremo— Velupillai Prabhakaran. He used human shields to defend himself and his remaining cadres as they were surrounded by the advancing Sri Lankan army on land and the navy at sea. Appeals from the Secretary General of the UN, humanitarian INGOs, and the temporary ceasefire by the government did not have him releasing the poor Tamil civilians held hostage. They were assisted to escape by the government army and navy and finally on 20 April, a fortification of the LTTE breached by the army had 35,000 civilians escaping to safety. But not before some were shot at by LTTE snipers and others killed in large numbers by Tiger suicide bombers who mingled with the escapees or invaded the refugee camps.

At the time of writing this revision, the government faces the triple task of countering international concern over a humanitarian crisis, the Tamil Diaspora in Britain, Canada, France and Australia demonstrating and calling for a ceasefire, as well as the rehabilitation of almost a million internally displaced refugees, and the reconstruction of destructed terrain. With international assistance this will be done. The

LTTE killed several Sir Lankan leaders including President Premadasa, who assisted it by driving the Indian peace keeping force back to India; Lakshman Kadirgamar, the country's most effective Minister of Foreign Affairs; Gamini Dissanayake and Lalith Athulathmudali—two potential leaders of the country; Neelan Tiruchelvam, a brilliant liberal Tamil human rights activist, and many others. One of the most shocking was the killing of Rajiv Gandhi, once Prime Minister of India and scion of the Nehru-Gandhi family, by a Tamil suicide bomber.

With the end of the war, the country looks forward to a period of reconciliation of the three major races, along with development and eventual prosperity.

A QUICK RIDE AROUND THE ISLAND

Sri Lanka calls itself the 'Paradise Isle' and not without some justification. In few other countries can one find such a variety of flora and fauna in such a small geographical location. There are basically three areas in Sri Lanka—the dry zone to the north and east, the wet zone to the south and west, and the central mountain area. It is a source of constant amazement to outsiders that each area is so different and that, when travelling in any one of these areas, it is almost impossible to visualise that another type of climatic area exists so close by. For instance, it is quite possible to drive right round the island without ever seeing a hill, even though the central part has mountains which rise up to over 2,500 m (8,202.1 ft). After a drive of approximately five hours from Colombo, the wilting temperatures of 33°C will drop to around 20°C in Nuwara Eliya. Night temperatures can go down to 6°C, the temperature that prevails in December through January.

The wet zone includes Colombo and the area that most visitors to Sri Lanka become familiar with. It is monsoonal territory and thus lush and fertile. The coastal strip that extends south from Colombo through the towns of Galle, Matara and Hambantota is like everybody's dream of a tropical island— deep blue seas, gently swaying coconut palms, picturesque little villages, all interspersed with dozens of hotels at which one can relax by a swimming pool or dip in the ocean. The majority of tourists who spend their vacation in Sri Lanka spend some, if not all, of their time in this part of the country, and local expatriates often make the trip down the 'Galle Road' to the nearby resort towns of Kalutara or Bentota for 'unwinding' weekends. When the south-west monsoon prevails from May through October and the seas are rough and dull in colour, the visitor could go to the east coast—Trincomalee, or further south, to enjoy a scintillating blue sea and stretches of water in Arugam bay that a child can wade in.

The tsunami of 26 December 2004 caused destruction almost all along the coast of the country, sparing only comparatively small sections along the western coast above Colombo. Lost lives of both natives and holiday makers, (December being the height of the tourist season) amounted to around 40,000. Many more lost their all. Economic loss was huge, since Sri Lanka was the worst affected country next to the Aceh Province in Indonesia. Reconstruction and rehabilitation are complete. Bigger and better hotels now dot the coastline.

Toddy and Arrack

One of the major activities on the south-west coast is the production of *toddy*. Early every morning and evening, selected agile men of the district, known as *toddy*-tappers, climb high into coconut or *kitul* palms to collect the sap which had been slowly seeping out from the tapped flower inflorescences during the intervening hours. Walking from tree to tree on specially strung tightropes, the *toddy*-tappers check the collecting pots that have been left there on their previous visit, and their contents are emptied into containers which they carry on their backs. This palm juice ferments very quickly, and is much sought after by the local villagers: in its natural state it is known as *toddy*, and is drunk rather like a weak beer, but after distilling it becomes known as *arrack*—the traditional spirit of Sri Lanka. Distilling *arrack* is strictly controlled and only the government and certain specially licensed companies are able to do it—although this does not always stop the production of local illicit brews, known collectively as *kasippu*.

The central mountainous zone is the tea-growing area of Sri Lanka. Climbing up from Colombo to Kandy, the road and the railway wind slowly up from the flat and humid lands below to the relative coolness of the hills until Kandy, the

home of the last Sri Lankan kings, with its central lake and famous Temple of the Tooth (possessing a relic regarded as a tooth of the Buddha), is reached. Climbing further up from Kandy, however, takes the traveller into the tea-growing areas and some of the most spectacular scenery to be seen anywhere in the world. From Kandy to Nuwara Eliya, the route goes through and above the dozens of tea plantations which are laid out like green carpets all around. At certain times of day, the traveller will see the brightly coloured *saris* of the tea-pickers who move methodically through the tea bushes, collecting the young top leaves of the tea bush for transportation to the tea factories located in strategic sites around the plantations.

At the summit of the climb through tea country, the town of Nuwara Eliya is reached, the focal point of the climb. It is here that the planters of old took their leisure. The Hill Club, redolent of the traditional British colonial image, still exists and is open for visitors to stay in; the racecourse, pride of the colonial community, is now being revived with horse racing after many years of abandonment; and the Botanical Gardens at Hakgala, second only to the huge and splendid one in Peradeniya, close to Kandy, provide a location for a hill country walk that is second to none. South and west of Nuwara Eliya, but still in the hill country, lies Adam's Peak, the sacred mountain; Horton Plains, with its scenically named World's End from which one looks down directly on to the flat plains 1,500 metres below; and Ella Gap, the gateway to the south, from whose resthouse one of the most spectacular views in the whole island may be seen.

The northern and eastern dry zone is probably less interesting scenically than the other parts of the country, because it is flat and rather arid. Little in the way of vegetation grows in abundance as it does in other parts of Sri Lanka; stunted bushes and the occasional Palmyrah tree are common sights while travelling through this part of the country. The agriculture practiced is *chena* cultivation—a slash and burn type of farming in which a small area is roughly cleared, set afire and then sown with cereal and vegetables. Once the harvest is gathered—often two rounds of it—the cultivators move on to another patch of land for the following season. This method of destructive agriculture, causing deforestation, is discouraged; *chena* cultivators are given land, both high and low, for paddy and other crop cultivation.

The most attractive features of the dry zone are to be found in the vicinity of the east coast beaches. Those who study such things often say that the sand and the sea are better here than on the west coast. The game parks—Yala specially—and bird sanctuaries in these areas are popular destinations of both foreign and local holiday makers. Jaffna, Trincomalee and Batticaloa are the regional centres of this area with Arugam Bay and Potuvil as excellent sea bathing beaches. The important historical sites of Anuradhapura and Polonnaruwa—with their ancient and complex solutions to the water supply problem still largely intact, and Buddhist stupas and temples—are also located in the dry zone in the North Central Province.

Whether coming to live or just to visit the country, the opportunities to travel and savour the mixture that is Sri Lanka are vast. Soon, like everyone else, the traveller will be overwhelmed that so much diversity can exist in so small an island.

The History of Tea

Tea was Sri Lanka's most important export, until the garment industry came into being with the open economy introduced in 1977, earning almost the highest foreign exchange. Tea remains, however, an important earner for the country.

Introduced by the British after a coffee blight killed off nearly all of Sri Lanka's first plantation crop, tea estates were laid out and first managed by the large tea companies who exported their produce to consuming countries. Superintendents of tea plantations: the senior *peria dora* and junior *sinna dorai*, were mostly Scottish and Irish. Nationalised in 1970–71, tea production came under the control of the Sri Lankan government's Estates Development Board, and tea was sold at tea auctions in Colombo to the distributing companies. Local planters took over from the British. Over 400 plantations are now managed by 22 private management firms, the transfer being effected in 1975.

The method of picking tea hasn't changed though: morning and afternoon, groups of tea-pickers (traditionally women, though there are a few men) fan out through the plantations, visiting each part of the plantation approximately once a week. Stopping at every bush on their designated route, they pick the young and tender leaves and buds—'two leaves and a bud'—of the new top growth. The tea is taken to the factory where it is withered on shelves with hot air blown through, rolled, dried and sifted into six or seven grades for sale.

Depending on the growing region, the most sought after tea is Broken Orange Pekoe and Fannings; the champagne of teas! Dust is another grade which is fine grained and gives a strong brew.

The refuse left after grading, comprising 2–3 per cent of total production, is denatured and spread in the tea fields as fertilizer. Apart from company tea plantations are small holdings which produce tea in privately owned factories known as 'bought leaf factories'.

Game Parks and Natural Reserves

There are 11 national game parks in the country and seven special bird sanctuaries. Of the former, Yala, Wilpattu and

Udawalawe are the best known and most visited. Kumana is a well known bird sanctuary in the south east. Due to LTTE incursion into Wilpattu game reserve, this area was depleted of its animals, even leopard and elephant, but was regained and restored in 2003. The most accessible and one of the most important is Yala Game Park in the south-east of the island. Within the park you need to travel in a hired three-wheel drive available at the gate, accompanied by a government Wild Life Department tracker. With a little bit of luck, the visitor will see herds of wild elephant, wild boar, deer, enough wild buffaloes to last a life time, myriads of different birds, and, for the very fortunate, a wild leopard or a bear. It is also possible, through prior arrangement in Colombo, to rent bungalows actually in the game parks where, if the visitor has the patience to stay put for two or three days, sightings of all the major Sri Lankan fauna are more or less guaranteed. Minneriya Reserve, near Polonnaruwa, is best known for its elephants, herds gathering in the vicinity of the Minneriya Wewa or tank, specially in September, when the dry zone gets parched with no rain until the North West Monsoon sets in November. Hundreds of elephants in their herds could be seen at this time.

LANKAN PROFILES

CHAPTER 3

'We shall in this part speake of the inhabitants
of this Country, with their religion and customs
and other things belonging to them.'
—Robert Knox

THE SRI LANKAN MOSAIC

The Sri Lanka of today is made up of a variety of ethnic groups that have combined with one another over the 25 centuries of the island's recorded existence, each adding a particular spice to the overall blend. Ethnically, however, this blend has not been achieved by a melting together of different ingredients into a new and transformed identity, but rather by stirring them together into a somewhat tenuous mixture which may or may not remain stuck together depending on how it is handled. There is overall harmony between races in 'Paradise Isle', and intermarriage does occur with some frequency, but there is no complete unanimity—and there lies the ingredient that threatens from time to time to poison the blend and make it separate into its components again. The blend if peaceful, however, adds greater spice to this 'spice island'.

The Veddhas

The original inhabitants of Sri Lanka, the Veddhas, are now very few in number. Their ethnic origins are undocumented, though they are believed to be descended from Indian Prince Vijaya and local Kuveni's two children. Successive waves of immigration and conquest drove them on to the eastern side of the central hills, where they are now concentrated in rural—and still fairly primitive—communities. The Veddhas have little contact with the other ethnic groups in Sri Lanka

A Veddha family. The patriarch, Tissahamy, sits with an axe on one shoulder, and a bow and arrows on his lap.

and tend to keep themselves to themselves, except in rare cases where intermarriage has occurred. Some were absorbed to village life, but most continued their traditional lifestyle of jungle living and hunting. Their lands were encroached on by colonisation schemes, so under their leader, Tissahamy, they even went to Geneva to demand designated territory to be called their own—a human right. This was granted by the Sri Lankan government and thus one sees them living in their own settlements in Dambanne, and other villages in the Uva province.

The Sinhalese

In 483 BC, a prince named Vijaya and 700 of his companions were banished from the kingdom of Sinhapura, which is presumed to have been somewhere in what is now Bengal, close to the present-day city of Kolkata (Calcutta). He was the son of King Sinhabahu and was exiled by his father. There is no record of why this was done—it may well have been that he felt he could do a better job than his father and had gathered 700 followers to prove it! Vijaya and his followers landed near what today is Puttalam, on the north-west coast of Sri Lanka. Legend has it that this arrival of the Indians was on the very day that the Buddha had his *Parinibbana* (death)

Vijaya took control and moved east-wards into the country. The original inhabitants either mingled with them or moved away into the hinterland.

The arrival of Vijaya and those who followed him created the nucleus of today's Sinhalese inhabitants. With them commenced the flowering of the ancient civilisations of Sri Lanka, centred in Anuradhapura and Polonnaruwa. Sinhapura passed into oblivion through that great shredder of nations, but the descendants of those Indo-Aryan settlers and the nation they started to build still remain—which goes to show that Vijaya must have had a point! The Sri Lankan flag has a sword-bearing lion in it. The animal represents the Sinhala race descended from the Lion Race. The minorities are represented by two broad bands on the side: green for the Muslims and orange for the Tamils.

Today, Sinhalese form 73.8 per cent of the population and are largely Buddhist, the religion that is followed by 69.3 per cent of the population. The remainder of the Sinhalese are Christians, by conversion originally during the colonial periods. They live in almost all parts of the country, but tend to be scarcer in the east and north of the country due to the ever increasing predominance of Tamil settlers in these areas. They were systematically ethnic cleansed from Jaffna and the Wanni in the last three decades, the latter being the stronghold of the LTTE. The LTTE indulged in ethnic cleansing and attempted dominance over the Eastern and Northern Provinces, and succeeded to a great extent in the North, from 1983 through 2009. During this period it was only the Sinhala soldier, sailor and airman, plus aid agency personnel and peace keepers (foreign) who were seen in the Jaffna Peninsula. With the final defeat of the LTTE in the Wanni in April 2009, it is expected that the Sinhalese and Muslims who lived in the North would go back to settle down in their former domiciles. The main road, the A9 highway from Kandy to Jaffna, being reopened after two decades of LTTE control and closure, will facilitate trade and travel. The Tamils, in contrast, were always able to live and work in any part of the country.

The Sinhalese are an easy-going, friendly people who are convivial on a casual basis, but much more reserved about entering into a more intimate friendship. Their language is Sinhala, an Indo-European language derived from Pali and Sanskrit. The letters are rounded and rather attractive to look at, but totally unintelligible to anyone brought up on a Roman alphabet system!

Talking to the Sinhalese is easy: almost any topic of conversation will do, and those that are usually avoided in Western society for fear of possible offence (especially religion and politics) are usually acceptable topics in Sri Lanka, as both are freely discussed among Sri Lankans themselves. Nearly everybody will want to know about you—where you come from, what you are doing, how you like Sri Lanka and so on—so starting a conversation should not be difficult, though it will often be somewhat superficial at first.

Sinhalese Names

Sinhalese names fall into two main categories: those of European derivation, adopted during one or other of the colonial periods (De Silva, Fernando, Perera, Dias, etc.); or those that are indigenous to the country (Premadasa, Ekanayake, Karunaratne, Ratwatte). In either case, most Sinhalese names end with a vowel rather than a consonant. When pronouncing them, all syllables are spoken separately with no silent endings (for example, Gamage is pronounced Gam-a-gay and not Gam-age). The 'gay' sound is, in fact, a traditional ending for Sinhalese family names.

The Tamils

Unlike the Sinhalese who are of Aryan stock, the Tamils are of Dravidian origin, and probably originated on the southern part of the Indian sub-continent. Also unlike the Sinhalese, there is no historical record or account of when they first arrived in Sri Lanka, but archaeological finds suggest that the first Tamil settlers must have arrived in Sri Lanka around the 3rd century BC. From that time on, there was considerable interaction between the Tamils and the Sinhalese, some of it positive but a lot of if decidedly unfriendly! Tamils held positions in the court at Anuradhapura and formed part of the army, but they were also frequently arrested and executed as traitors. Descendants of these early Tamil migrants tend today to live in the north and east of the country, where they are often referred to as Jaffna Tamils. Unlike in the north, however, the three races—Sinhalese, Tamil and Muslim—coexist peacefully in equal proportion along the east coast. The young radicals of the 'Batticaloe Tamils' (as the eastern Tamils are informally named) joined the LTTE and waged war, but were defeated since the eastern leaders, disillusioned with the LTTE Supremi, formed a new party and cooperated with the government. These breakaway LTTE are in the mainstream of politics and the Eastern Province is administered by a provincial council answerable to the central government in Colombo. The chief minister is an ex-LTTE cadre.

Much later, there was a second wave of Tamil migration, but for a totally different reason. In the 19th century, the British needed labour to work on the tea plantations. The Kandyan (Sinhalese) peasantry in the surrounding areas would not work on these plantations, firstly because they traditionally regarded themselves as farmers who tilled their own personal lands, and secondly because in any event, they considered it undignified to hire themselves out to foreigners. So the British imported labour for these plantations from their Indian empire (in the same way that they took Indian labour for work in other colonies), and thus increased the total Tamil population of Sri Lanka. These elements in the ethnic make-up of the country are known as Indian, or 'estate', Tamils and still tend to be concentrated in the hill country tea-growing areas.

Statistically, Sri Lankan Tamils amount to 13.9 per cent of the population, while Tamils of Indian descent number 4.6 per cent. The vast majority of Tamils are Hindus, while the balance are largely Christian.

The bulk of the Tamils being Hindus, a very rigid caste system exists among them—though notas rigid as that which still pervades Indian society. In this respect, it is very different from the Sinhalese caste system which, despite the break-up of the old socio-economic order, still

The language of the Tamils is called Tamil. It is a language of Dravidian origin, with its own distinctive script, much more square than round to look at, and is totally different from Sinhala—though just as unintelligible to the foreigner!

exists, originally based on occupation and which admits inter-caste marriage and is no bar to occupation or advancement.

Sinhalese and Tamils

Even though tensions between the Sinhalese and Tamils erupt sporadically and the terrorist conflict raged for 24 years, amity between the two races is also very evident. The seeds of the bitter conflict were sown by self seeking politicians— Sinhala, Muslim and Tamil—and fanned into flames by the LTTE. Basically the Sinhalese and Tamils work together and live beside each other. The Muslims are more insular and keep to themselves. Interracial marriages take place mostly between the Sinhalese and Tamil. These sometimes pose problems over family religion or traditions in bringing up children, but they are usually worked out quite simply and do not cause great consternation in the family or the community.

In fact, it is often a cause for puzzlement to the foreigner that, even though individual Sinhalese and Tamils, and groups in the farming community specially, can work and live so closely together, compromising fairly easily on their differences, their communities as a whole have not been able to do the same thing with similar ease. The racial split is mostly political, instigated by Tamil politicians and contributed to by Sinhala politicians vying for popularity with legislation like the Sinhala Only Act, which was abrogated. The LTTE propagated racial disharmony and waged civil war from 1983 until Prabhakaran and the remainder of his LTTE were vanquished by the government armed forces in April 2009. In the 1990s, having eliminated most other Tamil political parties or rendered them powerless, the LTTE claimed to be sole representatives of the Tamils, which was not so. It was the then President of the country—D B Wijetunge (May 1993–November 1994)—who significantly observed the on-going war at the time was not an ethnic war among the races of the Island but a terrorist war caused and perpetrated by the Tamil terrorists of the LTTE, adjudged to be the most ruthless of all terrorist organisations the world over.

There is little difference between Sinhalese and Tamils, however, when it comes to the art of conversation. Both groups love to talk to foreigners, and given a normal degree of tact, there are very few subjects for discussion that cannot be broached with either.

Tamil Names

Tamils, like Sinhalese, can be recognised by their surnames, which tend to end in a consonant, especially 'n' or 'm', while the majority of Sinhalese names end in a vowel. Many of the Tamil names are in some way associated with Hindu mythology. Variations on the name Subramaniam or Indran (both names for the second son of Lord Siva) are very common. Many others end with 'lingam'—Sivalingam, for instance.

The Muslims

During the Polonnaruwa period of Sri Lanka's history (roughly the 11th to the 13th centuries), trade in the Indian Ocean was dominated by Arabs. This trade flowed from parts of Europe, through the Middle East to China, and back. Sri Lanka, by its position, was an ideal entrepot for this ocean trade, which was part of the reason why south Indian states cast covetous eyes on the Island and invaded it from time to time. Sri Lanka attracted many foreign merchants and some even settled down in the island. The largest group among these were the Arab traders who, during the Polonnaruwa period, were believed to have been a dominant influence in Sri Lanka's international trade. As foreign trade grew in volume, these Arab traders appeared to have settled in growing numbers in the coastal areas and, naturally, around the ports.

As time went on, and the pattern and nature of this international trade changed, some of them moved into the interior of the Island and established themselves in local trade instead of foreign trade. This is why today there are concentrations of Muslims in the interior of the island, but considerably fewer in number than the large concentrations along the east, south and west coasts, in the areas of the old trading ports around which the Arabs originally settled.

A second group of Muslims arrived in Sri Lanka in the late

19th century. They were immigrants from the Malabar coast in South India, known in Sri Lanka as Coast Moors.

The Muslims of today have lost the pure Arab ethnic features of their ancestors, doubtless through centuries of intermarriage with the local population, as a result of which their distinctive features got submerged in time. The Muslims have maintained their identity, however, largely through their religion, and the customs and observances associated with it.

Muslim Names

Muslims can be recognised not only by their surnames, but also by their given names, which are of Islamic/Arabic origin. Apart from the Parsis, the Muslims are the only other group in Sri Lanka who have distinctive ethnic names, both given name and surname, like Mohammed and Ameer. Some Sinhalese and Tamil people use given names of Western origin.

The Muslims form 7.1 per cent of the ethnic population, but, in terms of religious belief, followers of Islam account for 7.6 per cent of Sri Lanka's population. This figure doubtless includes some Tamil Muslims. The word 'Muslim' in Sri Lanka is used to denote both the ethnic group (descendants of the Arabs) and the religious groups (followers of Islam). As can be seen, these do not necessarily coincide.

One of the older and more traditional mosques in Colombo.

Though descendants of Arab traders, Muslims in Sri Lanka do not use Arabic as the language of daily speech. Arabic is learned largely for Koranic studies and religious purposes. Muslims use either Sinhalese or Tamil depending on where they live, while some Muslims speak and use both languages.

The presence of a strong Muslim community in Sri Lanka can be seen everywhere. Mosques, the dominant architectural features of their surroundings, are common sights in all major towns, and Muslim communities in the countryside are easy to identify for the same reason. Because so many of the Muslims are still involved in some kind of trading activity or another, conversations on business topics and economic trends are always good icebreakers. Topics such as religion and politics sometimes need to be approached with a little more caution among Muslims than when talking to Sinhalese or Tamils. Be cautious also in dealings with Muslim women, who are considerably more sheltered than their sisters in the other Sri Lankan ethnic communities.

The Burghers

When the Portuguese and Dutch periods of colonisation ended, not all the Portuguese and Dutch left Sri Lanka. Those who stayed behind included people who had married into the local community. Their descendants are collectively referred to as Burghers. The word is the same as the Germanic word used to signify the middle-class occupants of a city, and is a reference to their urban rather than rural origins.

The Burgher Story

The Burghers of Sri Lanka may be the only group of people in the world who came into existence as citizens of a particular town rather than of a particular country. Born as offspring of Portuguese or Dutch fathers and local Sinhalese mothers, these racially mixed children were not eligible for the citizenship of their fatherlands, nor were their mothers able to offer any citizenship by their own right. In a typically Sri Lankan compromise, this unclassifiable and stateless group of people were awarded the citizenship of the town in which they were born (hence the term Burgher), and they were only later given citizenship of Ceylon/Sri Lanka. But the title 'Burgher' stuck, and the Burghers of Sri Lanka are today proud of their ancestry.

The Portuguese Burghers have largely found themselves concentrated over the years in Batticaloa and a northern section of the city of Colombo, Kotahena, which was once a very elite residential area. Over the years, large sections of it have been overtaken by commerce, industry and the Port of Colombo, yet areas still exist which are residential and still retain their old colonial charm.

The Portuguese Burghers have always been a small community with a *joie de vivre* of their own, and have retained among them their old traditions of food, dance and song. Indeed, a whole lot of their popular tunes, known collectively as *baila* (Portuguese for dance), is a *sine qua non* as a conclusion to many a Sri Lankan party—formal or informal—sung to words which have been written for it, or even made up in the inspiration of the moment. The traditional dance forms that originally accompanies this music are rarely performed, though some steps are improvised at these get-togethers. Formal dinner dances and informal parties invariably include "sessions of *baila*" where traditional Portuguese dancing steps are executed with or without partners of the opposite sex.

The Dutch Burghers have largely found themselves concentrated over the years in Matara and in a southern section of the city of Colombo—Bambalapitiya and Wellawatte. If the descendants of the Portuguese have maintained the gregarious nature of their colonial antecedents, the descendants of the Dutch have maintained the aloofness of theirs. During the British administration, while the positions at the higher and mid-administrative levels were held by Europeans, clerical posts were held largely by Burghers of Dutch descent. In the railways, the drivers and guards of trains were drawn from among the Burghers, mostly the Portuguese Burghers who worked hard and drank hard! There were Dutch Burghers in the professions as lawyers and doctors—some of whom were there during the agitation for self-government. Latterly, when the higher levels of administration were opened up to Sri Lankans, there were many Dutch Burghers who entered these ranks.

In the post-1956 period, the large majority of the Dutch Burgher community felt unhappy with the changes that

Sometime early in this century, the Dutch Burghers formed the Dutch Burgher Union, where membership was open only to those who could prove, through their family trees, they were direct descendants of the Dutch colonisers.

were taking place and migrated, mainly to Australia. There were those, however, who stayed behind and have, over the intervening years, contributed in no small measure to the development of the country.

Burghers form around 0.2 per cent of the population today, and they are all Christians. Although usually—but not exclusively—of Dutch or Portuguese origin, they have always spoken English, which they consider their mother tongue. Like the other ethnic groups in the country, Burghers can be recognised by their distinctive surnames, many of which, such as Bartholomeusz, Direckze or Loos, reflect their European heritage.

The Parsis and Borahs

The Parsis and Borahs are very small communities that came, comparatively recently, from India. Parsis are Zoroastrians— fire-worshippers—by religion, and must have been of Persian origin as the name Parsi suggests. Though a small group, they have made a name for themselves as professionals and business people over the years. The Borahs are also mainly in business and are Muslim by religion.

The Malays

Malays are another very small community, of Malayan origin naturally, who came to Sri Lanka during the British period. They are Muslims by religion. They are to be found in all walks of life, though many are engaged in trade.

The Europeans

The Portuguese were not the first Europeans to come to Sri Lanka. Marco Polo, the Venetian traveller, claimed to have been here, and long before that, Pliny the Younger records an embassy from the king of Sri Lanka to the Roman Emperor Claudius.

There must have been trade and other contact between the West and Sri Lanka in times predating colonisation. The map of the world which Eratosthenes drew in 220 BC (over three centuries before Ptolemy's of 150 AD) has a fairly accurate depiction of India and Sri Lanka (Taprobane, as it was then known), but it is only with the Portuguese and the Dutch that we find persons of European origin settling in Sri Lanka in any substantial numbers.

In the 19th and early 20th centuries, once again many Western travellers passed through Sri Lanka. Among them were figures as diverse as Colonel Henry Olcott the Theosophist, who played a significant role in the Buddhist revival in the country, Mark Twain, Somerset Maugham and Lord Mountbatten of Burma, who spent the World War II years in the island as commander in the South East Asia Command (SEAC), when allied troops in their numbers were stationed in Colombo and Kandy.

During the period immediately before independence, another European contact of a very significant nature was also made. The *Mahavamsa*, the work which relates the early history of Sri Lanka from a Buddhist standpoint, was first translated by a German, Professor Wilhelm Geiger, and, as a result, there has since been considerable German interest in Buddhism. Sri Lankan *vihares* were set up in Germany, and a German Dhammaduta Society exists in Sri Lanka. Interestingly enough, tourist groups who visit the island tend to be more often than not from the German-speaking countries! That is until the Japanese, Chinese, Indians and other Asians were enticed to visit Sri Lanka.

In the post-1948 period, there have been Westerners and their descendants who have stayed on or settled down in Sri Lanka. There are still a few British planters, businessmen, British Council officers and descendants of the British (known as Eurasians as distinct from the earlier Burgher), and even some other European nationalities (German and Italian, for instance). Other Westerners, who have married Sri Lankans and settled down with them in the country, are still in evidence. Numerically, however, they are fewer than the Parsis or Malays. Sri Lankans take pride in the fact that Sir Arthur C Clarke, renowned scientist, science fiction writer, inventor and futurist, settled down in Colombo in 1956 mostly due to his love of scuba diving, and integrated himself happily with the Sri Lankans. He was much respected and was appointed Chancellor of the University of Moratuwa, which has the School of Computer Science bearing his name. He was also conferred the highest national honour—*Sri Lanka Abhimanya*. His death on 19 March 2008 was mourned by Sri Lankans as the demise of a loved and respected friend of the nation.

THE SRI LANKAN SOUL

Sri Lankans are some of the kindest and friendliest people in any country in the world. As individuals, whether they be Sinhalese, Tamil, Muslim or Burgher, they are hospitable and outgoing with a keen curiosity about the world around them. The foreigner walking the streets of Colombo, or any other major Sri Lankan city, will often be asked where he is from and be engaged in conversation by people eager to find out more about his country. Of course, on some occasions, this questioning does have an ulterior motive, for Sri Lankans are also quick to see an advantage for themselves—if there is one—in any encounter, but most of it comes from a genuine desire to be friendly.

Religion and the family play a major part in the lives of Sri Lankans, and tradition exerts a strong influence over both. Certain patterns of behavior and ways of thinking come from these traditions and the fact that foreigners do not believe the same things or act in the same ways as they do is sometimes a source of amazement—especially in the rural areas. By and large, Sri Lankans are a conservative people who have to

judge for themselves whether a difference is automatically an improvement or not. Thus change comes slowly in the country as a whole; it is sought and constantly implemented to improve the public lot, but the private lives of the people often change little even though their circumstances or their location might. Globalisation has, however, wrought much change. One example is that few women now stick with the traditional *sari*; dresses and suits are worn even to work, leaving the *sari* for formal occasions.

Sri Lankans, however, are quick to anger. As in many tropical countries, tempers are never very far below the surface and often become apparent when transgressed. Sometimes, among themselves, an outbreak of temper can take a very violent turn, but in everyday life, their volatility manifests itself nowhere more obviously than in the way that they drive! Also, as Sri Lankans are individually volatile by nature, Sri Lankans in groups are often even more so— rallies, demonstrations and meetings sometimes sound as though World War III is being declared! However, the heat of the group dissipates quickly in most instances as the participants revert to their individual personalities, away from the presence of their peers.

One transgression, however, is never pardoned—no Sri Lankan of any persuasion appreciates being regarded as an ethnic Indian: Sri Lankans are fiercely jealous of their nationality and their separate identity. On a closer acquaintance with Sri Lankans, the foreigner will see that this is indeed so, as beliefs and traditions are different, and ways of seeing not the same as a result.

The Sri Lankan personality is a complex one—often quiet and reflective, sometimes hot and irritable, occasionally even violent. They are loyal to what they believe in, and accept foreigners willingly and for what they are, but with a strong sense of pride in their own identity.

Another national trait that is apparent during elections is the political bent of all Sri Lankans—they are indeed political creatures! Politics and what members of the ruling party are up to and, of course, gossip about VIPs are priority topics of conversation whether in an elite city drawing room or village tea boutique.

SOCIALISING WITH THE LOCALS

'Among the people there are divers and sundry Cast or degrees of Quality, which is not according to their Riches or Places of Honour the King promote them to, but according to their Descent and Blood... but to take a more particular view of the State of this Country, we shall first give some account of their religion, and then of their other secular concerns.'
—Robert Knox

WAYS OF SEEING

The Sri Lankan has a perspective on life that is all his own. Forged partly through his social background, partly through his religion and partly through his fierce addiction to politics, his way of seeing is a combination of all three which sometimes makes for great insights into universal problems and sometimes results in tremendous conflicts of beliefs and loyalties.

Tradition is the only unifying factor in Sri Lanka and as this slowly and inexorably breaks down under the pressures of the modern world, the Sri Lankan seeks new ideas and concepts which will enable him to come to terms with what he sees happening around him. Sri Lanka is a changing society—a lot of the old ways have already disappeared and have been replaced with imported Western customs—but it is still a fundamentally stable one and, both in towns and villages, the concerns that really matter and have proved most valuable still endure, and will continue do so despite influences that may overlap them and attempt to obliterate them.

Village and Town

In spite of its comparatively large cities, Sri Lanka has never really been a country with a strong urban mentality. Nearly three-quarters of the population live in the countryside, which is as it should be as the island's economy is more agriculture-based than industrial. Even those who live in the city and its suburbs often feel the same way about their small community as do their country cousins.

Traveling around the country, you will know when you are nearing a village or settlement—even though houses may not be immediately visible as they are often screened off by trees and bushes—by the clustering along the roadside of a number of small shops. The number of these shops, their size and the manner in which they are constructed and stocked will tell you something about the size of the village and its relative affluence. At a minimum level, you are likely to find one general store which stocks the daily necessities of the residents, while in a more affluent village, there will be a number of small speciality 'boutiques' as well. Every village, no matter how small, will also have an eating house generally called a *buth kade*, literally 'rice shop', and a *te kade* (tea shop) and *kopi kade* (coffee shop). The latter two are meeting places for the men of the area, usually in the early evenings, for a brew of tea, a chew of betel and a chat. Foreigners may feel like steering clear of some of these places because of their exterior appearance, and avoid buying anything from them (except perhaps bottled stuff) in deference to their stomachs, but some—especially those at which the long distance buses and trucks stop—serve excellent local food (spicy and hot) as well as very well-brewed tea.

In both villages and small towns, the inhabitants are unfailingly helpful and friendly to anyone passing by who may need assistance, and no one need really worry about being stranded in Sri Lanka. This friendliness, however, will rarely be extended to an invitation to spend the night or to share a meal. This is not because the Sri Lankan is in any way xenophobic, nor is it simple inhospitality, but a genuine worry about how a foreigner would react to his lifestyle. Most houses tend to be sufficient only for the family living within, and both food and sleeping arrangements may be much more basic than a foreigner is accustomed to; so to avoid awkwardness, don't expect helpfulness to extend beyond what is necessary, unless it is a dire emergency or you have gotten to know the family very well.

A foreigner appearing in a small community would not, however, be treated as a strange phenomenon or considered a superior being. Foreigners have stayed in villages and have been surprised at the equanimity with which they have been received by all the villagers and the immediate acceptance that they have been granted—word soon gets around on the village grapevine whose friend they are and where they are staying.

It is a great mistake to underestimate villagers in Sri Lanka: they are not a low social stratum, and even the most obtuse of visitors cannot help but be impressed with the basic and inborn dignity of the true villager. It was Knox who, noticing this feature or phenomenon, said that any cultivator from a Kandyan area could be taken from his fields, given a good wash, dressed in royal robes and enthroned, and he would fittingly look and act king!

A very common and typically Sri Lankan sight to be seen while driving through the countryside—or even in the small communities on the edges of towns—are groups of people bathing themselves and washing their clothes at a standpipe, a common well, a stream that passes by, a river, a *wewa*, an irrigation channel or, in the hill country, simply a spout that sticks out from the rock wall itself from which clear sparkling water gushes out. Bathing is a very dignified process, and very much a part of the integral daily routine. Mornings and evenings are the time for the men, before and after their daily work, while the daytime is for women and children to bathe, often as an offshoot of doing their family laundry, washing their cooking utensils or collecting water from the well.

The Sri Lankan takes his bath by pouring water over his head from either bucket or pot—often the shiny aluminium pails that are used to carry water from the well to the home—or, if in a stream or canal, by submerging himself repeatedly, often accompanied by a sweeping hand movement and a loud hiss or sigh. Soap is very much a part of the process— the highly soaped bodies of bathers are a common sight by the wayside as the bath progresses. The men bathe in shorts, G-string or sarong tucked up, while the women wear a *diya redda* (literally 'water cloth') wrapped tightly around the body at armpit level and reaching down to the ankles, somewhat like a Western woman's wrap-around bath towel.

A group of *diya redda*-clad bathers, shy but happy to be photographed.

The difference is that once the *diya redda* gets wet, it clings tenaciously, attractively sculpting the wearer. After the bath is the time for gossip, exchanging the news of the day or catching up on the latest installment of a long-standing dispute.

Animals too are washed in the same way, and it is a common sight to see bullocks and elephants wallowing contentedly in the local stream or river, while having their backs scrubbed vigorously by their employers. *Mahouts* (men who are in charge of elephants) in particular, often earn a fair day's money at bath time from camera buffs who stop, stare and click away at the great beasts lolling on their sides, splashing themselves by siphoning and swooshing water over themselves with their trunks.

In fact, the truly urban Sri Lankan is a relatively rare bird. In the largest cities such as Kandy and Colombo, the standard and style of living is decidedly Western, as are the pastimes and the social events organised and patronised by those who choose to live in a Western style. But ask any Sri Lankan where his native village is and he will be able to tell you—the village is never far away from the city, even in the minds of those whose bodies now enjoy the luxury of houses with modern conveniences and air-conditioned cars!

Caste

The attitude towards caste is perhaps one symptom of the traditional thinking that characterises even the most Westernised of Sri Lankans. Although caste no longer officially exists, and many Sri Lankans will tell you that it is no longer a factor in the life of the country, there are still occasions within each ethnic group when subdivisions relating to caste or racial descent are evident. For instance, the Burghers who have no caste system still demarcate themselves into two groups: those descended from the Portuguese and those whose Dutch heritage is so important to them that there still is in existence an exclusive Dutch Burgher Union.

The Jaffna Tamil considers himself superior to the Batticaloa Tamil, and both adhere to a caste system of the four main castes, with further sub-castes: Ksastriya (ruler), Brahman (religious leader/priest), Vaisya (cultivator) and Shudra (manual worker/labourer). Adherence to tradition occasionally manifests itself in a situation where a high caste Tamil might feel impelled to refuse to work under a lower caste one, whatever the latter's seniority might be.

Caste is no longer nearly as pervasive among the Sinhalese as among the Tamils, and there are very few occasions when it will even be noticeable to the foreigner. One way in which the Sinhalese do still divide themselves is into two main social groups: the Kandyans—those from the hills—and the low country Sinhalese (Uda rata and Pahatha rata).

There is a tendency for the Kandyans to regard themselves somewhat as the aristocrats of Sri Lanka, because of their descent from the last of the indigenous kingdoms, while the Portuguese influence on the low country Sinhalese is clearly evident from their names, many of which were adopted during the Portuguese period. Perera, Mendis, de Silva and Fernando abound as surnames of the low country Sinhalese while the Kandyans often have names unpronounceable by the foreign tongue, derived from the name of their ancestral village. The two groups are also recognisable by the manner in which the women drape their *saris*, and their general complexion. The Kandyan woman is fair of face and modest, wearing her *sari* in a distinctive style while her darker sister from the lowlands drapes her 5 metres in the Indian manner.

The only place in which caste still really plays a dramatic role in Sinhalese contemporary society is in the arranged marriage market. The three qualifications or prerequisites stipulated in proposed marriages are caste, religion and family background, with affluence or earning capacity a close fourth. Advertisements in the Sunday newspapers ask for brides or grooms as marriage partners for 'Well connected doctor—MRCP, Kandyan Govigama Buddhist'. If the seeker of a marriage partner is emancipated (or desperate), the advertisement will read thus: 'Caste and religion immaterial'. The man who has a skeleton in his bachelor cupboard may stipulate 'a silent wedding preferred' where silent means a quiet, no fuss, not pre-advertised ceremony.

Marriage Partners For Sale

The Sri Lankan Sunday papers are still widely used as a medium to advertise for prospective marriage partners. These pitches for partners range from the sublime to the sad to the ridiculous, but they are all intended to be taken seriously. A sampling from one week's edition:

- Aunt seeks for niece, 39 years, Govigama Buddhist drawing a salary over Rs 20,000, a suitable partner below 45 years. Write with copy of horoscope and other details. Caste, race, religion immaterial.
- Catholic Govi parents seek for fair, good-looking accomplished daughter, 28 years, a suitable partner. Dowry cash one million. Other castes considered.
- High caste Hindu parents seek suitable partner—doctor or engineer—for their English-educated, very fair and beautiful daughter, age 26. Considerable dowry in cash, property and jewellery.

A website on the Internet now acts as matchmaker and a couple of ladies who are into this business computer match the applicants. Most marriages, however, are arranged informally through mutual friends or aunts. More than half the marriages that take place are so called love marriages.

I FOUND YOUR FATHER THROUGH AN ADVERTISEMENT. LOW MILEAGE AND GOOD CONDITION

Although among the Jaffna Tamils caste still remains important and is still tacitly acknowledged, in other areas of Sri Lanka, it is now largely the happy hunting ground of sociologists seeking subjects for doctoral theses; and acknowledged when marriage is considered. It is not a subject that should exercise the mind of the foreigner unduly.

The Sinhalese Caste System

The caste system among the Sinhalese has its origins way back in the monarchical history of the island. The stratification was according to the trade, craft or profession followed from generation to generation.

Thus you get the Govigama caste high up on the hierarchical ladder, the descendants of landowners and cultivators. Of them, some are Radala, i.e. connected to the aristocracy of yore. The Karava are fisher folk, while the Salagama were originally cinnamon peelers. The Hakuru crowd were *jaggery* makers (*jaggery* being the candy made by heating and stirring the sap collected from the inflorescence of the kitul palm, a species of coconut). Berawaya were and still are *tom-tom* beaters (drummers) and Paduva were *palanquin* bearers—very low on the caste scale. Radhau are washer folk, and the lowest of the low are the Rodiya, very recently rehabilitated and educated. They were, and many still are, itinerant gypsies; the men recognisable by their stock-in-trade—either a wicker basket of snakes, mercifully defanged, slung on one shoulder, who emerge and slither around as the owner plays his fat-bellied flute, or a dressed up monkey on a leash who performs according to commands given him. The Rodiya woman is similarly unmistakable. Tall, well proportioned and poised, she has her thick, luxuriant hair tied in a *konde* (top knot) high above her neck. Rodiya women, whose usual means of livelihood are palm reading and singing, are dark skinned and very attractive, but were not allowed inside home gardens for fear of charms and abduction.

In fact, in rural homes of the well-to-do, where traditions were clung to, the Rodiya was not allowed anywhere near the house. Low benches were placed for lower caste persons to sit on. Padu women who came to the *walauwes* (homes of the high caste) were not allowed to wear blouses but had to make do with a cloth tied across their chests, this as recent as 60 years ago in Kandyan villagers. The picture mercifully has changed dramatically. You could very well find an educated Padu person holding a top job today, although a person of a higher caste will still think thrice before he runs a launderette or takes to drumming on the traditional *bera*.

Caste used to raise its head during elections when the caste of a candidate is discussed if it is 'low'. A Karawe would vote for a Karawe. But this is no longer so. Now, with the voter being a more sophisticated party man, it's the candidate's party that matters, not his caste.

Buddhism

Buddhism is a very important factor in the daily life of approximately 70 per cent of the island's population. It was introduced to Sri Lanka three centuries after the Buddha's death, by King Asoka of Mauryan repute. The *Mahavamsa*, the original Buddhist history of Sri Lanka, records that, around 250 BC and at the request of King Devanampiyatissa of 'Jambu Dvipa', King Asoka sent his son Mahinda, along with five ascetics, to the island. The king, while hunting deer, met Thera Mahinda in Mihintale, a couple of kilometres away from the capital city, Anuradhapura. With the first sermon

The Buddhist temple is an integral part of every village, along with the irrigation tank and paddy fields. The stupa, or *dagoba* shown here is one component of a typical temple, the others being a preaching hall, a *vihara* housing statues, a bo tree and the abode of the monks.

preached by Mahinda, the king became a Buddhist, the Thera being satisfied with the king's intellect and the king having gauged the depth and value of the new religion. Soon Buddhism spread all over the country and received royal patronage.

Shortly after, a second message was sent to India, since Queen Anula wished for ordination for women. This time,

Two young devotees in a temple on Poya day.

King Asoka sent his daughter Sanghamitta, a nun, who arrived in Anuradhapura bearing a sapling of the very tree under which Gotama Buddha attained Enlightenment. The sapling planted with pomp in the centre of the city still grows in Anuradhapura, distinguished as the longest living, historically authenticated tree.

Sri Lankan Buddhism is the Theravada form of the religion, its scripture and rules being those laid down by the Buddha and passed down the ages unadulterated and devoid of ritual. In fact, much of Sri Lankan culture—painting, sculpture and literature—owes its inspiration to the ideas and precepts of Buddhism.

Buddhism today, though not a designated state religion, wields the most influence in Sri Lanka. All the prime ministers and five presidents of the country have been Buddhists. The Sangha (Buddhist clergy) stayed clear of politics. The Mahanayakes (head priests of the three sects) act in an advisory capacity to the rulers, from earliest times to the present. Political leaders often pay their first visit after election to prestigious posts, to the Temple of the Tooth and to the two Mahanayakes resident in Kandy.

The three sects of *bikkhus* (monks) in the country stress the strict observance of the *vinaya* (rules as set down by the Buddha) to keep clear of involvement in lay life of the land. But once in a while, they do step into the political arena as happened prior to the presidential elections of December 1988. The JVP (see Chapter 2: Overview of Land and History on page 15), within whose ranks were young monks mostly from the universities, almost succeeded in paralysing the country by calling for *hartals* (stoppages of work, transport, government business and so on). When the crisis reached near unmanageable proportions, the Mahanayakes called strongly for the dissolution of parliament and the holding of presidential and general elections. They were placated but not heeded instantaneously. The Sangha had, in 1998, categorically objected to the joining of the northern and eastern provinces, as proposed in the government's devolution package and much else in it as giving too much to 12 per cent of the population.

In the run-up to parliamentary elections in April 2004, a group of Sinhala nationalists, with Buddhist monks joining in, formed a party known as the Jatika Hela Urumaya. Nine monks were voted in to Parliament, with the stated purpose of cleansing the seats of power of corruption and excess. They were subsequently reduced in number to seven. Their influence in the political arena has been greatly reduced. Liberal Buddhists are against monks being in active politics, having to face the indignity of hurly burly politics. Their contention is that the place of the monk is in the temple, seeing to his own deliverance from rebirths and guiding the supporters of the temple to lead better lives.

Other Major Sri Lankan Religions

Although it is the largest, Buddhism is by no means the only religion practised in Sri Lanka—a country which prides itself rightly on the freedom it gives to worshippers of all faiths.

For example, the many waves of invasion from south India that flowed and ebbed across northern Ceylon have left their imprint on the sands of time in the form of Hinduism. The majority of Tamils in Jaffna, the eastern coastal belt and the highland tea country are Hindus, and the sight of highly decorated *kovils* (Hindu temples) with their tall *gopurams* is a common one all over the island.

So it is with mosques. Arab and other West Asian traders introduced the Muslim religion to the island, and the Moorish sculpture of cupola dome and filigree trellising separate the mosque from other buildings. Their existence points to the fact that there are adherents of the religion of Islam all over Sri Lanka, and their festivals are very much part of the traditions of the country.

Western colonisation of the island, missionary activity and the Westernisation of a substantial segment of the elite grafted Christianity in its various forms of worship and ritual on both the Sinhalese and Tamil races in the 16th to 19th centuries. Thus it is mostly in the maritime provinces and in and around Colombo that Roman Catholic, Anglican, Methodist and Baptist creeds took hold. Concrete evidence of this can still be seen in the huge and ornate Catholic churches that dominate areas which were under Portuguese control, and in the smaller, parish-church style buildings dotted throughout the tea plantations in the hill country.

Conversion both by conviction and coercion occurred so that Buddhism hid its face before the onslaught of Christian crusading. There is actually some evidence to show that Christianity existed in the country long before the coming of the Portuguese. Excavations at Anuradhapura (one of the foremost ancient cities of Ceylon) produced a cross which is believed to be the form used by the Nestorian Christians.

An Anglican church with modern architecture.

Hence the surmise is that a Christian settlement was a certainty in ancient Sri Lanka.

Recently, there has been the advent of other forms of Christian worship such as Jehovah's Witnesses and Born Again Christians. These groups have converted Buddhists and Hindus to their form of worship by capitalising on the people's poverty and offering inducements such as free milk for infants, text books, even nursery schools being built and staffed, and of course, money payments. Condemned by the Buddhist clergy and the traditional, established churches, people were made aware of the danger of coerced or persuaded-by-bribes conversion. An Anti-Conversion Bill brought in by the JHU did not go through its three readings in parliament and has been, mercifully, dropped. The monks have been convinced, or at least told, that legislation is not the way to stop such malpractices, but that greater concern shown to poor villagers and the disadvantaged in towns will curb forced/induced conversions.

A recent phenomenon is the fellow-feeling forged and exhibited by the various religions. No important event, such as the commissioning of a multi-purpose reservoir or declaring a new school building open, for example, is celebrated without dignitaries of the four major religions being in the VIP enclosure. Cross invitations are extended and accepted so one sees Buddhist monks in church and Hindu swamis side by side with Muslim religious leaders.

Adam's Peak: a stiff, steep climb up to a footprint at the summit.

The Story of Adam's Peak

Even in myth and legend of times long past, the conflicts that shape Sri Lankan history can be seen in all their glorious confusion. For example, the third highest mountain in Sri Lanka—Sri Pada or Adam's Peak—is regarded by all as a sacred place to be honoured and venerated, because deeply indented in the rock at the top of this 2,200-m (7,217.8-ft) peak is an imprint that looks remarkably like a footprint. But no one has ever been able to agree on whose footprint it is, or symbol of whose, since it is outsized and cannot by any means be a human footprint. The Christians and the Muslims say that it is Adam's, placed there on his expulsion from paradise; the Buddhist Sinhalese say it is Buddha's, placed there on his third visit to this Island, while the Hindus claim that the great Hindu god Siva, when visiting this insignificant island, left his mark on the top of this remarkable mountain.

Warning: Avoid Religious Offence

Buddhist places of worship are treated with care and respect. One would on no account enter a place of worship with one's shoes and cap on. Women should be appropriately dressed, so avoid mini-skirts and short shorts please! Sleeveless blouses are also frowned upon, so take a shawl with you if you are dressed for the heat. In the Temple of the Tooth in Kandy, recognising 'tourist dress code', sarongs are handed over to

Elephants at work or at play can often been seen in Sri Lanka. Here, they immerse themselves in a river for an enjoyable bath after a day's work.

Sri Lanka has many festive celebrations due to its multi ethnic and multi-religious community Here, a Buddhist procession known as a *perahera* goes underway.

Fishermen pull their boat up onto a beautiful beach in Uppuveli. Fish and other seafood is an abundant natural resource in the waters around Sri Lanka.

Shopping is a crowded affair on the busy streets of Colombo.

Visitors make a steep climb up Adam's Peak in central Sri Lanka, atop which is an imprint that many consider to be a sacred footprint.

both men and women, so that you could be in your mini-skirt or shorts but still be temporarily suitably leg-covered.

The Buddhist priest has a special place in Buddhist society, being one of the three elements of veneration—the Buddha (teacher), the Dhamma (doctrine or teaching) and the Sangha (the priesthood or monks). In a temple, one does not engage a Buddhist priest in general conversation as one might a Christian priest in the parish church. However, if the priest speaks to you, you would naturally respond. This does not mean that you should not initiate a conversation. Ask questions, make conversation, but with a certain amount of deference, and about the religion, history of the temple, the country et al.

Buddhist priests do not attend social functions. They do come to homes for occasions revolving round religious observances or on invitation to discuss the Dhamma. The chanting of *pirit* (the Dhamma in stanza form as preached by the Buddha in Pali and handed down generation to generation) and the acceptance of *dana* (alms) are two occasions on which monks would come to a home. These are usually to confer blessing on the home or an inmate, or to commemorate the anniversary of the death of a loved one.

Foreign guests are often invited to such occasions. They are not expected to join in the religious observances, which entail the monks being seated on low sofas or cushions placed on the ground and covered over with white sheets. An almsgiving is full of ritual, but once the monks have departed, the occasion turns into a happy lunch party.

The contact of the Buddhist monk with women is kept to the barest essential minimum. It would not be advisable for non-Buddhist women to deal directly with Buddhist monks unless it were for instruction or to discuss the Dhamma or meditation practice.

The thinking behind this is definitely not anti-feminist. It is in deference to the monk withdrawing himself from lay life and the need for one who has renounced ordinary life to be exposed as minimally as possible to attractions of the world; so there is conscious distancing in view of the Adam and Eve syndrome. Foreigners who travel in public transport will observe the reservation of seats for the clergy. If there are no priests in the bus, the seat can be sat upon; but the moment a monk enters, the seat must be given up, the woman passenger being the first to do this.

There are sometimes religious ceremonies in the workplace. Participation by adherents of other religions is not expected and is not obligatory. If it is the opening of a new office and your presence is called for, you just being there would satisfy the organisers.

It must be mentioned here that the lighting of the coconut oil lamp, the beating of drums, the boiling over of a pot of milk or the consumption of milk rice on auspicious occasions are not religious in nature any more than the Christmas tree or the Easter egg are. They are merely traditional accompaniments to significant events. Religious observances on such occasions involve the chanting of *pirit* by Buddhist monks. Where a ceremony of this nature is held in a temple, participants wear white or simple light-coloured clothes.

There is another aspect of religion, particularly pervasive in urban settings, which needs special awareness. You should not expect anything to be done by a Muslim on a Friday mid-morning as that is his prayer time, nor would a devout Buddhist have much time to spare for you on a Poya day (*see* Chapter Seven: Enjoying Sri Lanka *on page 131*).

Religion is a touchy issue the world over, and in spite of the demands of normal urban life in Sri Lanka, it is still very much part of the individual culture.

One important point needs to be clarified.

The foreign visitor, having seen the many Buddhist temples, the oversized Buddha statues, the joss stick and flower-crowded altars before the bo tree (*ficus religiosa*) and the *dagobas* (huge dome-like constructions often housing relics of the Buddha or of his disciples) may get the idea that Buddhism is ritualistic, a religion of prayer and faith or the worship of several gods. Nothing could be further from the truth. No Buddhist is expected to worship or even venerate the Buddha as Almighty God the way Allah or the pantheon of Hindu gods are worshipped.

Buddha showed the path to *nirvana* (deliverance from an unsatisfactory state and the cycle of rebirths), and he is The Teacher, not by any means a god or super-human. Statues are for the simple in mind, the less philosophical. To get a picture of true Buddhism, speak to a monk or accost a Buddhist lay person on his way to temple for a day of observing the eight precepts and meditation and you will get your questions answered.

Hindus keep their religious ceremonies to themselves except their *vel* festival. Here, a highly decorated cart carrying a statue of a Hindu god is taken from one *kovil* to another. En route the procession stops at homes, shops and business establishments irrespective of race or religion, disbursing holy water and ash.

Orthodox Hindus shun tobacco and alcoholic drink and do not eat beef. (They may wink at a drink or enjoy a cigarette but will not desanctify the cow whom they hold sacred.)

Muslims keep religious ceremonies and prayer sessions exclusively to themselves. They are forbidden by Koranic law to eat pork, smoke and take alcoholic drinks. (The latter two vices are sometimes indulged in, much to the displeasure of their womenfolk and the censure of Islam.)

Local Christians are generally no different in their practice from Christians the foreigner would meet in his own country.

Politics and Pragmatism

The Sri Lankan is highly conscious of politics, occasionally too much so. Indeed, it has been said that if you get three Sri Lankans together, you will find them forming four separate political parties!

Part of the reason for this is the high level of literacy in the country and the large circulation of newspapers in the three languages, and also the ubiquity of radio and the rapid inroads made by television.

Most important though, is the fact that democracy is nothing new to Sri Lankans. In ancient times, life in the village was democratically ordered, so this form of behaviour has existed at grassroots level for a long time. Voter turn-out at elections has always been very high, and the turn-out at the presidential and general elections held under very difficult circumstances in December 1988 aroused worldwide acclaim as the Sri Lankan voters braved the threat of the gun to preserve their democratic rights.

Polls have degenerated in the recent past, with vote rigging and thuggery scandalising the north-west provincial elections in January 1999. This situation improved with poll watchers or election monitors, both local and foreign, touring the land.

The worst happened during the presidential elections in November 2005. No votes were cast in Jaffna and surrounding areas held by the LTTE or adjacent to its territory. This, it was argued, lost Ranil Wickremasinghe the presidency, since he was the candidate who would get the votes of minority groups. Mahinda Rajapakse's election as president was said to be due to the LTTE's veto, its threatened avoidance by the people of all polling booths in the north. Only two persons braved the LTTE command and cast his/her vote, with reportedly dire consequences.

The foreigner will hear and see much in the political arena but had best not involve himself too intimately. Let the heated arguments rage, the very last thousand rupee note wagered, the hair of the head shorn off by the loser of a political bet, but let it all go without comment.

One small extra word of caution may be necessary for the foreigner, however: over the years, politics has crept into the administration of the country, with political appointments being made at numerous administrative levels. The foreigner might need to be aware that the official with whom he has to deal would be a political appointee; though to put the matter in perspective, the vast majority of civil servants are still apolitical.

Political Parties

Political parties in Sri Lanka range from the right of centre to the left, and nearly all the parties cut across lines of ethnic origin, social class and religious belief.

Some of the exceptions to this are the Tamil parties—the Democratic Worker's Congress being totally comprised of Indians from the plantations—and the Muslim Congress, which is restricted to the believers of Islam. The oldest political party is the UNP (United National Party) while the principal party in the coalition in power since April 2004—the SLFP (Sri Lanka Freedom Party), has the distinction of having elected the world's first woman prime minister in 1960 (Mrs Sirimavo R D Bandaranaike).

Of the two political parties that considered the bullet more effective then the ballot—namely the Liberation Tigers of Tamil Eelam (LTTE) in the north and the Janatha Vimukthi Peramuna (JVP) in the South—the LTTE was defeated in May 2009, since calls by the government for it to lay down arms and join mainstream politics were rejected many times over. The JVP leadership was decimated by the then UNP government in 1989, and peace was restored in the island, barring the north and parts of the east. The JVP is now a mainstream political party, while the LTTE was proscribed consequent to its guilt in the assassination of several Sri Lankan politicians and India's former prime minister, Rajiv Gandhi. The proscription was lifted in November 2001, and a peace pact signed by the LTTE Supremo, Velupillai Prabhakaran and Prime Minister Ranil Wickremasinghe. The LTTE however did not lay down its arms; rather it used the period of negotiated peace to reinforce its army and navy. It avoided peace talks during the presidency of Mahinda Rajapakse (2005–) and re-engaged government forces in

Eelam War IV, before finally being defeated completely in May 2009.

At the parliamentary elections in 2001, a party comprising Buddhist monks and a left-leaning party was forged. Eight monks of the Jathika Hela Urumaya were elected to parliament.

SOCIAL ETIQUETTE

All this having been said, on the surface, Sri Lanka might appear more akin to the society from which the foreigner has come than it is in reality. The apparent veneer of Western sophistication, conspicuous in the cities although less so by degrees in the small towns and villages, is often only skin deep. At one end of the spectrum, the foreigner will find the 'hail-fellow-well-met' type of Sri Lankan whose enthusiasm for all things Western knows no bounds, while at the other end can be found the conservative traditional type. The variations in between are considerable.

A rule of thumb for all might be to start formally without being too distant or too friendly and gradually thaw out. To start off with plenty of bonhomie, being everyone's friend, is an obvious mistake, and although most Sri Lankans are too polite to criticise directly, it could lead to the formation of great reservations about your sincerity.

Relationships with women are another consideration. In Sri Lankan society, a man's relationship with a woman is always formal unless they are blood relations or have known each other for some time. In a village, the social structure itself makes sure that this rule is followed, but in the apparently more relaxed urban community, it is easy to make a *faux pas*. On the whole, married women are far less protocol-conscious than the unmarried, in whom both mothers and the norms of society have drummed the fact that modesty and reserve are valued qualities in young women.

Certainly in the villages, and to a great extent still in the towns and cities of Sri Lanka, life moves at a calmer and slower pace than it does in most other parts of the world. Foreigners should be patient if things do not always go with the utmost efficiency and speed because, although the pace is leisurely, things do eventually get done. If you ask someone to do something and it is not completed on the dot, keep calm—it will be done and usually quite well.

On the whole, foreigners are welcomed and made to feel at home. There is seldom any alienation, though there is a consciousness that no matter how long you stay, you will never think or feel exactly as a Sri Lankan does. The Sri Lankans know this and will make allowances for your errors and enthusiasm, so that it is possible in time to become close friends of the kind in which cultural gaps can be bridged with a willingness to understand on both sides.

One word of warning: an over-achiever coming to Sri Lanka would do well to bear in mind the epitaph written for one such as he: 'Here lies a man who tried to hurry the East' remains today a good cautionary message to many a modern Westerner working in, or visiting Sri Lanka—whether he is businessman, a development consultant, a tourist or even a recluse seeking his own *nirvana*.

So tread carefully and develop your own perspective on the country amid the joyous melee of caste and creed, political affiliation, exoticism and friendliness that is Sri Lanka and enjoy its beauty—both of the land and that inherent in its people.

THE LIFE CIRCLE

'...it is time to return home to our lodging.
And the night coming on,
we will lead you to their bed chambers
and show you how they sleep.
About which they are not very curious.
If their house be but one room (as often is) then the men
sleep together at one end and the women at the other.'
—Robert Knox

The Modern Family

Time was when large families were the order of the day in Sri Lanka. Dwellings were spacious, gardens were large, life moved at an easier pace, and there was time to slow down without the fear that inflation or some other economic monster would devour your earnings.

The pace of life is quicker now, though not yet as overwhelming in its speed as it can be in the West. Aspirins are still used for the occasional headache; tranquillisers have not yet come into common use.

Successive administrations have embarked on programmes of family planning (a concept that has been well received in Sri Lanka), the numbers of working parents have increased, and with the growth of employment opportunities in local industry or abroad (particularly in the Middle East), the availability of household aides has been reduced. All these factors have contributed in some measure to the arrival of the smaller family in Sri Lanka. Muslims do not favour limiting their families, particularly through birth control methods.

The Importance of Being Born

The birth of a child is an event of major importance in the family. So much so that, in the not so distant past, if the first child was not born within a year of marriage (the nine-month deadline was decidedly preferable), it was widely thought that there had to be something wrong with either the husband or the wife (depending on whose family did the speculation).

Today, couples plan their families and generally keep them within the limits which allow equal treatment and equal opportunity to all the children within the constraints of life.

Everybody, friends and relations alike, visit the mother and the new baby, either in the maternity hospital itself, or soon after the mother returns home. Visitors bring a gift for the baby—something the child can use or play with. Gifts are generally not given before the child is born. Baby girls are given jewellery by close family and good friends, perhaps bangles or a set of earrings, which the mother keeps until the child can wear them.

The Role of Astrology

Astrology plays a significant part in the life of any Buddhist or Hindu. Any important event is governed by astrology.

The astrologer will not only pick out the auspicious day for a function or other event, but even the exact time at which proceedings should begin. Among Buddhists and Hindus therefore, it is quite common to find that when a child is born, the date and exact time are noted, and an astrologer is asked to cast a horoscope for the child. A horoscope highlights the major events and periods, both good and bad, throughout the person's life. Horoscopes were inscribed on ola leaves, which are then retained in scroll form. It's more likely the astrologer will now give the parent charts drawn on a paper. Keeping up with the electronic age, horoscopes are computer cast, mostly for children born to expatriate parents, where the time of birth is first converted to standard Greenwich time and then to the local Sri Lankan time.

Astrologers are also consulted for specific advice on the auspicious day and time on which to embark on an enterprise, conclude a deal, get married, lay the foundation stone for a house or building and any other event in one's life which one might consider important. In a Sinhalese arranged marriage, the horoscopes of the bride-to-be and groom-to-be are compared by an astrologer. If at least 10 of the 20 *porondan* (features) are compatible, the proposal will proceed and the two will be married, if the young ones agree to it. If even one of the astrologers consulted by each party decrees the horoscopes do not agree, the matter will be dropped forthwith.

Childhood Rituals

The first ritual of childhood is generally the prerogative of Muslims and is known as the naming ceremony. Forty days after the birth of a child, the family gathers together and in their presence, the *imam* from the family mosque names the baby, whose head has been especially shaven for the event, by whispering the chosen name three times in each ear. Circumcision, required by the Islamic faith of all males, is

A traditional horoscope bearing the astrological chart inscribed on ola leaf, which rolls up to form a scroll.

also often performed at this time, but more generally when a boy is around 12 years of age.

The next important event in a child's life, regardless of its religion, is when it takes its first solid food. Generally, a family elder who is considered fortunate with children feeds the child its first mouthful of rice (the staple food) with the gravy of a bland curry (one that is not heavily spiced and certainly has no chilli in it). This, and other similar events, are more social and symbolic in nature and have no deeper significance. For instance, if the child finds the first mouthful of rice unpalatable, it is no omen that it will grow up into alien food habits and live on a lifetime diet of fish and chips, Kentucky Fried Chicken, or even *chappaties*!

In Sinhalese families, the first feeding of rice to a baby is ritualistic and done at an auspicious time, having an astrologer read the mite's hosorcope. *Kiributh* (milk rice), *kavun* (oil cakes, a traditional sweet), a book and a gold chain are placed on a mat, and the kid will then be carried onto it. If he grabs the food, he is destined to be a glutton; if the book, a scholar; and if he goes for the gold, he will be rich and prosperous in life! The mother usually watches with bated breath, since any wrong doing of a kid is blamed on the mother, or her genes!!

The learning of letters is another important event. Again, an elder would take the child through reading and the motions of writing the first letter—a symbolic launching into the world of formal learning. In Buddhist families, it is often the temple priest who does the first teaching. If the child turns out to be a poor learner, it is no reflection on the elder concerned, or the manner in which that first letter was formed.

Birthday celebrations are an imported Western custom and not everyone celebrates a birthday. When it is done, it takes the same form as it would elsewhere in the world—cakes, candles, gifts, games and fun.

Coming of Age

Growing up is of more significance to women than to men. In more sheltered homes and conservative families, the daughter stays in her room or the house for the duration of her first period. It is considered inauspicious for the girl to see male members of her family and other males, of course, until she has her ritual bath. From then on, right through life, baths are not taken during this time. In fact, some women are brought up so conservatively that they will sleep separate from their husbands during their menstrual periods. These practices do not necessarily occur only among rural folk, nor are they confined to any particular ethnic or religious group, nor do they hold the sanction of invariable custom.

Sinhalese families make a ritual of the first bath after the first menstrual period. The *dhoby* woman (washer woman) pours a clay pot of water over the young girl very early in the morning. With the demise of the *dhoby* in cities, supplanted by washing machines and launderettes, grand aunts willingly perform this task. The water has jasmine flowers in it. The girl then looks into a bowl of water with floating jasmine, and blows out a *lit pahana* (oil lamp). She then eats *kiributh* and *kavun*, and reverts to normal food after having been served bland, meatless food during her period.

Celebrations in the way of parties are held by some to mark the coming of age. In olden times, it was a sort of announcement that here in this family was a marriageable daughter. Even now in villages, grand parties are held, more as an excuse for partying and to collect gifts! Among the gifts a girl might receive at this time would be jewellery from parents, grandparents and even close friends of the family. Others invited to the party would bring gifts of a general nature.

The rite of passage of boys is less dramatic and generally not specifically acknowledged. Muslims perform the circumcision ceremony at this age, if it has not been performed earlier. In most societies, there is little in the way of formal initiation into manhood.

Betrothal and Marriage

Marriages in Sri Lanka may or may not be arranged. In the past, the marriage broker played an important part in most marriages (whether in the role of the formal matchmaker, or in the form of one who merely 'spoke' on behalf of one party o the other). Today, however, more and more young people choose their own partners.

There are three 'social' functions surrounding the event. The first is the engagement, the second the wedding reception and the third the homecoming.

However, it should be pointed out that every marriage would not necessarily consist of all three functions, and the scale on which they are held varies. Some might limit it to family and relations only, some extend it further to close friends, and some go further to include acquaintances as well. Some would even prefer to get married quietly without any of these functions.

Though there could be three celebrations round one event, a gift is usually given only once—habitually at the wedding reception. If for some reason you have missed the wedding, you could take the gift along to the homecoming (if invited to it), or have it delivered. The American practice of showers for the bride-to-be is not generally known in Sri Lanka.

Wedding Invitations

Invitations are specific. Invitations to the wedding reception are formal, printed ones. Invitations to the engagement and homecoming could be formally printed or verbally extended by the principals or their parents, but all of them would be specifically directed to the persons expected. Sri Lankans are generally informal and it could happen that, at an informal party, they turn up with a friend (usually after prior arrangement with the host, if that is possible), but this would not apply to the functions surrounding a wedding.

There is no hard and fast rule about wedding gifts. Usually, the gift is some item of general household use or an ornament which is sensible without being extravagant. Gifts of cash are also given. Unless you are related to the bridal couple or know either or both of them or their parents very well, and can afford it, your gift would not go into the costly range of things like TV sets, stereos, expensive kitchen or household appliances or furniture. However, if the office or unit where one of the persons works can collect enough money for a collective gift of this nature, then it certainly would be welcome.

In offices, a party could be given to a person who is to be married, shortly before he or she goes on leave prior to the wedding. This would usually take place during working hours in the latter part of the working day. The occasion could be used to give a collective wedding gift from the office. If the wedding is within office hours, then be prepared either to work very short-handed, or to close the office or unit for half a day or more to enable colleagues to attend the wedding. This would include time to go home and change into clothes for the wedding, and get back home after the wedding to change into working clothes.

A wedding is an occasion for dressing in one's best—particularly for the womenfolk. In the past, a wedding meant a new set of clothes for everyone in the family, but the inverse relationship between wages and prices today no longer permits this except to some very fortunate persons. However, brand new or not, you wear the best you have to the wedding; for women, the most colourful and expensive of *saris* and the best jewellery. The clothes worn to the engagement and homecoming would be somewhat less dressy, as would the jewellery.

Men would wear lounge suits or safari suits to a wedding. To the engagement or homecoming, slightly more casual dress (shirt and tie) would be permissible, though if the functions are held in a public place like a hotel, a suit would again be appropriate.

If the functions are held in a private hotel, there would be a time constraint. If they are held in a private house, however, they could go on almost right through the night; Sri

Christian marriage ceremonies (and often those of Hindus) take place in a place of worship. The religious ceremonies of marriages of other religions are performed in the home or at a public place like a public hall or hotel banquet room.

Lankans love parties of all sorts and enjoy merrymaking.

The serving of liquor at these functions is a matter of choice. Muslims and Parsis, for instance, as a rule will not serve any liquor. For receptions in houses, glasses containing alcohol will not normally be carried round on trays like the soft drinks. They will be located on a table on which the mixer will also be placed, and the men help themselves.

Music is an indispensable accompaniment to any private function in Sri Lanka, whether it is a small party or a large reception. It includes both Western and Sri Lankan popular music. In rural areas, the music is amplified through loudspeakers so that everyone knows that there is a celebration going on. In small communities, everyone is generally asked to a wedding. The festivities can last from morning to evening with people dropping in at will.

After the wedding come the wedding visits. Previously, the newly-weds were expected to visit all those who came to the wedding or sent gifts. But that was in the days of leisure, and today they can no longer do it, nor is it expected. However, the newly-weds will visit members of the family and some close friends. In the usual manner of social visits in Sri Lanka, these are not pre-arranged, and they just drop in. If they don't find anyone at home, they will try again later.

The Buddhist Wedding

At the central point on one side of the marriage room is the structure called the *poruwa*, which symbolises a home. This consists of a square platform beside which, at the four corners, are four pots filled with coconut flowers, in each of which is placed a lighted *pahana* (clay lamp). There is a canopy of flowers or some rich material over the platform.

The bride and groom stand in the centre of the platform. The ceremony commences at the auspicious time. A master of ceremonies chants religious stanzas (Buddhist priests do not officiate at Buddhist weddings). A sheaf of betel leaves is given to the groom by the master of ceremonies and the bride and groom offer it to their parents. Rings are exchanged, the groom places an expensive necklace around the bride's neck, and presents her with a rich *sari* and blouse for her "going away" after the wedding ceremony.

The bride and groom feed each other with a piece of milk rice. The little fingers of the left hand of the bride and the right hand of the groom are tied together with gold thread and water poured over their fingers from a silver goblet by a maternal uncle of the bridegroom, symbolising future prosperity.

Young girls in white *saris* sing *Jayamangala Gatha* (verses to wish blessing and prosperity on the couple), and when the singing is over, the groom hands each one an envelope with money in it. A coconut is cracked with one sharp blow of a knife as the couple descends from the *poruwa*. An expert is commissioned since the way the coconut cracks is portentous, two perfect halves denoting a very successful and happy marriage. The bridal couple then signs the register at a table prepared, at which sits a representative of the Registrar-General.

After this formality, the couple sits down on a sofa specially prepared for them. Toasts are drunk if so desired and the reception gets under way. The guests make their way to the bridal couple and congratulate them.

If there is dancing, the bridal couple leads the way onto the dance floor. Needless to say, there is dancing at these functions only among the Westernised segment of urban society.

The parents of the couple mingle with the guests, speaking to each and every one, as do the couple.

Parenthood

The married couple does not live entirely on their own and by themselves. They are part of a family, and family ties in Sri Lanka are still strong.

People keep physically in touch with members of their own extended families fairly regularly. So, when children are born, the elders are there to provide the support that is needed—especially the wife's mother to whom she naturally turns to. Thus, from the start, the infant has more people in its circle than the parents. There are the grandparents, and the uncles and aunts too ... and even beyond that!

It is customary for the mother and the womenfolk to take care of the infant. Not too many husbands in Sri Lanka would brave a change of diapers with infant legs thrashing in the air in energetic abandon. The burdens of office and the stresses of business and profession are almost a welcome refuge from bringing up children. Sri Lankan mothers generally breastfeed their infants, and the legally stipulated period of maternity leave for working mothers (which is obligatory and binding on employers) is ILO decreed: three months. In estates and other places of work, a mother is given two leave breaks of an hour each to go nurse her baby. This is succinctly called the *kiri paeya* (milk hour).

It has been suggested that the male attitude of infant caring being a female prerogative is derived from chauvinism or some kind of feeling of male superiority. The truth is simpler; the job is left to the partner who can do it better.

Possibly derived from this concept is the traditional 'drawing of lines', so to speak, between the parents. The mother looks after the home; the father is the provider and the one who deals with outside affairs when the need arises. The child gets its view of, and ability to deal with, the outside world from its father; from the mother is received emotional stability and spiritual growth. This is not invariably so, and the mix can be in varying proportions, but this is the overall pattern.

Growing Old

In the traditional Sri Lankan family, growing old holds no fears. It is the time when, after a life of work, you take a couple of steps back and watch the passing scene—as the cliché goes—and, more importantly, have your family care for you, in one way or another.

But this is not a negative existence. The younger generation go to elders for advice on the larger problems and issues that face them, to benefit from their knowledge of the world and experience of its ways. However, there is no formal position that elders have in a family, and generally youngsters have their own favourite elder or elders. Elders must also be invited to all family functions—if the children or youth find this a problem, the parents usually ensure that it is done.

One thing which has not changed is that elders are not neglected or cast aside. Someone in the family takes them in and looks after them. Even when they decide to live by themselves, others keep in regular touch. They are not put in institutions of old age homes unless there is some compelling reason for this.

This is the reason why homes for the aged or institutions of that nature are not developed in Sri Lanka as they are in the West. Indeed, if an elder is put into such an institution, the implications are either that there is no family member to look after the person, or that no family member is willing to look after the person or able to do so. In either case, there is somehow a sense that a social norm has been broken.

Death and Dying

There being many different religions followed in Sri Lanka—added to by a sprinkling of atheists, agnostics and rationalists—diverse customs prevail with regard to death. But in general, serious illness and death are matters of concern not only for the whole extended family, but also for friends and acquaintances.

If a patient is seriously ill, relations and friends will visit him whether in hospital or at home. Indeed, if a person is hospitalised, relations and friends will visit him regularly, regardless of the gravity or otherwise of the illness. Hospitals in Sri Lanka are crowded during visiting hours, and members of the family might even take regular home-cooked meals for the patient—as 'hospital food' is a term that is uncharitably used for bland, unpalatable cooking. Others might take something on their first visit (some fruit perhaps, or flowers), but this is not necessary. What is expected is a visit.

The thought of friends and relations milling around a sick bed could raise eyebrows in some quarters, but it surely raises the patient's spirits to have around him reminders of his daily life. It makes him feel that he has not been cut off from it.

A business boss may or may not visit a co-worker or employee in hospital, depending on the closeness of the

office relationship between the people working there. Just one visit should suffice in this instance. If a visit is not convenient, a get well card or a similar gesture would be appropriate.

A funeral draws everyone who knew the deceased and who is able to be present. The obituary notice over the radio and/ or in the daily newspaper, or a message conveyed about a death, is an intimation that you should attend the funeral if the deceased was known to you. In Sri Lanka, people may, for example, attend the funeral of a friend's parent even though that parent may not have been known to them. Of course, foreigners would not be expected to do this, unless as a gesture to a particular friend.

The body lies in the house of the deceased or immediate family member, or in a funeral parlour until the time of cremation or burial. It might be mentioned, though, that Hindus and Muslims invariably keep the body in a house and not in a funeral parlour. Throughout this time, relations and friends keep constant vigil by the body, right through the night/s as well.

There are two things to be done in connection with a funeral. One is to visit the house or the funeral parlour, and the other is to attend the funeral itself. It should be noted, however, that for Muslim burials, only male relatives accompany the body to the cemetery. Also, if it is the practice to remove one's footwear before entering the room where the body lies, this should be done.

Muslims bury their dead in shallow graves within 24 hours of death; Hindus cremate theirs; and Parsis have a Tower of Silence. Buddhists generally cremate their dead, while Christians may either bury or cremate them. For cremations of all faiths, the gas crematorium has today largely replaced the funeral pyre, and only the distinguished, the very wealthy and the very traditional still use pyres made of logs of wood. Time was when the ashes retrieved from the cremation were interred in a public cemetery or a private, family burial ground, with a considerable amount being spent on a headstone. Many express the desire that their ashes, gathered after cremation, be scattered in a river or the sea.

Then, the matter of dress for funerals. Men used to wear a white suit (generally cotton) and a white shirt with a black necktie, and women invariably wore white *saris* or dresses. You might notice, even today, men of the older generation dressed in this fashion, but as a rule, men no longer wear coats to funerals. The shirt could be white or grey, or perhaps even a light cream. The trousers could be of any sober colour. A black necktie is generally worn, though. Women wear white, though sober shades of grey and blue are also seen.

Wreaths are not commonly sent today. In the case of an office worker or member of his immediate family, a collection may be taken for a collective wreath which will usually be carried into the house or funeral parlour and placed by representatives from the office. Alternatively, since it is often specifically mentioned 'no flowers by request', the collected money is donated to some charity specified in the death notice or given to a close relative to be spent for the seven day's *dane* (alms giving) in the case of a deceased Buddhist.

MEETING THE LOCALS

Sri Lankans are a very social people and entertaining is very much a part of their culture. The socialising that is mainly done, however, is of the more informal kind—not pre-arranged—involving either friends and neighbours dropping in for a chat over a glass of whatever brew happens to be handy, or going out to some kind of social gathering in the community, such as a fair or public entertainment.

In keeping with this informality, many a friendship has developed over the garden wall in Sri Lanka—if your garden wall is not too high! Unfortunately, most Westerners tend to live in houses that are well isolated from theirneighbours by high walls and in some cases by security guards, and thus meeting the neighbour is actually quite uncommon. For this reason, the Sri Lankan friends of expatriates tend to be made through other means such as in the workplace and in social clubs. However, neighbours will generally be friendly and ready to talk, so if you are short of a cup of sugar…

Incidentally, when meeting someone, be aware that shaking hands is not a Sri Lankan custom, although it is the most common form of greeting and reciprocation to being introduced. On formal occasions the greeting '*Ayubowan*' might be used, accompanied by a hand gesture in which the palms of the hands are placed together in front of the upper chest in a praying posture. However, this would be considered quite out of place in a more relaxed setting where the tendency is simply to say '*Kohomada*', the Sinhala equivalent of 'How do you do?'.

Hopefully, the time will come when a formal invitation is extended to visit a Sri Lankan home for a meal or an evening with friends. Remember, however, that most Sri Lankans are very informal and entertaining reflects this. Rarely will a tie be worn to go out—only on the most formal of occasions and even then traditional Sri Lankans will tend to wear their own national dress—and attire can be quite casual, providing the excesses of beachwear are avoided. If the invitation is for dinner, remember that many Sri Lankans eat very late, and that the time for which one is invited will have been expressed in the Sri Lankan time frame rather than in a Western one. Dress codes are stipulated in formal invitations, the most common being 'lounge or national' and of recent origin, 'smart casual'. The former means a suit and tie or the national costume of white or cream cloth with a tight necked shirt or Indian *sherwani*.

GIFT-GIVING

Rules governing personal gift-giving are substantially the same as they are in any Western country. It is appropriate to give gifts on birthdays and festivals—such as Christmas for instance—and small tokens of appreciation are always appropriate among friends on special occasions. It is not expected to take the hostess a gift when invited out to dinner, but is usually done. A bottle of wine does not go amiss, providing, of course, that the hosts are not Muslims. Flowers, fruits or other stuff like tins of biscuit or boxes of chocolate are also much in vogue.

Gifts are given to servants and employees either at Christmas or at the local New Year in April, and usually take the form of money, often a predetermined bonus of a set amount. For instance, one month's salary is common for domestic employees. Regular callers at your house, such as the postman and garbage collector, also receive some form of financial gift at this time of year, the amount depending on the service rendered and how often. Don't worry about having to remember to do this; they will not be backward in coming forward and asking for it with lists! However, make sure that it is well known when you give such gifts—otherwise you may find that you are asked for them more than once during the year.

To Tip or Not to Tip?

As in many Western countries, there is no hard and fast rule about tipping. A service charge of 10 per cent is added to the bill in almost all restaurants and is non-negotiable. An extra few rupees if the service has been particularly good is also appreciated, but not mandatory. Tipping is not expected in some places where one would think that it might be—such as to taxi drivers. The man who pumps air in your tyres, for example, would naturally appreciate a tip.

SETTLING IN

CHAPTER 5

'This after some time made them change their minds
and not to think of themselves as Slaves any more,
but the Inhabitants of the land to be their Servants,
in that they laboured to sustain them. Which made
them begin to Domineer, and would not be content unless
they had such Victuals as please them, and oftentimes
used to throw the Pots, Victuals and all at their heads
that brought them, which they patiently would bear.'
—Robert Knox

THE EXPATRIATE EXPERIENCE

Expatriates in Sri Lanka occupy a very special position in society. Even though a part of the daily life of the country, they can never really become Sri Lankan because their background and experience are alien to the background and experience of the people around them, even though superficially there may appear to be many points of similarity. Living in a large house, employing servants, belonging to the most expensive clubs, and using such appliances as air-conditioners immediately set them apart from all but the most affluent few of those they live among.

It is extremely difficult, but not impossible, for expatriates to become accepted by Sri Lankans as anything other than foreigners who, because of their work, happen to live in the country for two or three years. The question must be asked, of course, whether the foreigner actually wants to be accepted on the same terms as a local, and whether it is even appropriate that he or she should be.

THE RESIDENCE VISA

Every foreigner residing in Sri Lanka longer than the period of time allowed to a tourist for a visit (usually one month) has to obtain a Residence Visa or Work Visa. The expatriate arrives on a landing visa and the institution/firm that employs him/her will obtain the Residence Visa for him/her.

To quote from the website of the Immigration and Emigration Department of Sri Lanka (http://www.immigration. gov.lk): "To obtain a Residence Visa, it is necessary to arrive in Sri Lanka on an Entry Visa issued by a Sri Lanka Mission abroad with the concurrence of the Controller of Immigration and Emigration, Sri Lanka. A Visit Visa issued without the Controller's approval will not be considered for conversion into a Residence Visa."

This Residence Visa has to be renewed annually. The cost of a Residence Visa or its renewal in 2009 is Rs 20,000.

This visa, which equates itself to a work permit is useful for a number of reasons: obtaining a reduction on the usual tourist rate in several resort hotels, obtaining other permits such as a Sri Lankan driving licence, and generally clarifying one's official status when called upon to do so in security-conscious Sri Lanka.

One word of warning, however: do not go on leave without ensuring that your Residence Visa will still be valid when you re-appear at the airport. Failure to do this could lead to a lot of unnecessary complications.

HOUSE AND HOME

An expatriate coming to live in Sri Lanka will normally be placed in one of two positions as far as finding accommodation is concerned. Either the company for whom he works will provide him with a house, or he will receive an allowance to rent one.

Rentals in the sought after areas of Colombo (Colombo 7 and 5) are quite high—usually in the range of Rs 75,000 to Rs 125,000 per month—and houses may come furnished or unfurnished, depending on what is needed. Rental rates in other parts of Colombo and in other towns are lower, but the quality of the accommodation is likely to be lower as well. Many new pricey high-rise flats are now available in Colombo.

If a house has to be chosen by its occupant, there are several things to watch out for.

The first is the method by which it is selected. This can be done through placing or answering an advertisement in the newspaper, through friends, or through an estate agent.

The latter way will be the most expensive, as estate agents often receive a commission from both the landlord and the tenant, but the least trouble.

When actually looking at a prospective house, check that if the house is not centrally air-conditioned, which some of them now are (such a house is prohibitively expensive if you are paying your own electricity bill), the rooms are large and airy with high ceilings for maximum ventilation. It is customary to have large ceiling fans in each room to provide air circulation, and certainly these are a boon on hot sticky days that haunt Colombo in April and early May.

If you plan to have live-in servants, the house should also include their quarters, usually a standard feature in older houses. Most houses in Colombo have very little in the way of gardens and are surrounded by a boundary wall, both to demarcate that property from the neighbours' and to provide security. If you are lucky enough to find a house with a garden, be sure to check where the trees are located. Too close proximity to the house can mean problems with blocked gutters and drains, as well as providing easy access to the upper floors for the curious.

You will usually find that the windows in all of the rooms have metal grilles on the outside. If by a small chance they are not a feature of a chosen house, these should certainly be added, as they provide the opportunity to open the windows for fresh air without also inviting the neighbourhood to come in through them! Kitchen windows should have fly screens in addition.

You should also check the condition of the roof: houses with asbestos roofs tend to be very hot, while the traditional tile roofs are much cooler.

One further factor to keep in mind when selecting a house in Sri Lanka: it will be almost impossible to escape from the animals that live in them as well. The little gecko that runs freely about the walls in search of insects is quite clean and harmless and offers no threat at all to the occupants unless it gets into food or is boiled or cooked with what you take! It is supposed to be poisonous then. Cockroaches are a little more unpleasant, but are equally persistent until matched with a determined effort at extermination, which will usually reduce their numbers! Repellents are effective. Air-conditioning or fans at full blast and sleeping under mosquito nets will keep mosquitos at bay.

Furniture

Furniture is fairly easily available and sturdy, though not of the type that a Westerner might be used to. Most furniture in Sri Lanka is slightly uncomfortable by Western standards, being designed more to be functional and suitable for the climate than for decorative purposes and cosy comfort.

Avoid heavy, overstuffed furniture which tends to be very hot unless the room in which it is placed is always air-conditioned. Traditional Sri Lankan pieces of furniture, such as those items made of cane, are among the most practical to use in the house, as are the traditional individual styles of chair, such as the *hansiputuwa* (also known as the Planter's Chair) with its long curved back for reclining and its extension for resting tired feet.

Telephone

Most services should already be connected to any house you are provided with. If you rent your own home, make sure that it has a telephone already installed, as paper work is necessary otherwise. It is possible to have a telephone with an overseas dialling facility in it, on payment of a fee. Payphones are freely available at supermarkets and even road sides, with easily bought phone cards for amounts ranging from Rs 100–Rs 1,000. These cards can be used with your telephone too. Calling countries such as the US, UK, Japan and India are almost the same price as calling within the country. (Rs 20 or cheaper per minute). Mobile telephones are ubiquitous. At least four companies vie with each other; hence, facilities and repair services are prompt and costs comparatively low. The telephone system in the country is privatised and hence efficient service is available from SLT—Sri Lanka Telecom.

Internet facilities are readily available from Sri Lanka Telecom and others, with broad band in Colombo. It is possible to get 'light surfing' facility for as cheap as Rs 287 per month.

Public Utilities

Water supply should be fairly constant—except in times of drought when water rationing is brought into effect—though some areas do have problems with low pressure due to the extreme age of the supply pipes! One precaution is worthwhile. Your house should have a water storage tank and this should be kept full at all times to provide water in the event of water cuts. Better still, have an underground sump and overhead tank.

Electricity should similarly be no problem, but be a little cautious about arranging to live in a house outside municipal limits of Colombo in areas where urban councils see to amenities. Problems with equipment service facilities result in power breakdowns and cuts more often than they otherwise might—and usually at times when they are most annoying. Sudden surges could also affect electric appliances.

Emergency Services

Most emergency services have contact numbers that are manned day and night, and most of them are quite quick to respond. The police will respond fast if their central number is called and the local police station is not too far away, as will the fire brigade in Colombo; though be aware that they only have one station and it may take them a while to get to you if the roads are congested.

For medical emergencies, it is best to call your doctor directly and make arrangements to meet him at a hospital. If this is not possible or if you have no immediate transportation, calling the Red Cross ambulance service, which has trained attendants to take you to the nearest large hospital, is probably the best alternative. Most private hospitals or nursing homes have their own ambulances. There are also commercial services such as Red Alert and Medicalls which will provide a doctor and/or emergency transportation to its members for the price of a phone call and an annual subscription fee.

For power failures and water failures there are central numbers to telephone. In my experience at least, they were found to be usually quite quick to respond and efficient when they arrived; even if their repairmen did come by bicycle!

Security

With the defeat of the LTTE, bombs and suicide bombers are evils of the past. Violence is a presence but not of the destructive kind, particularly to expatriates who are not into politics et al. However, security is a major issue in Sri Lankan homes at the moment. While Colombo is generally a safe city to live in, and it is unlikely that you will be physically in danger, burglary and petty theft are quite common and security precautions are definitely in order.

Two such devices, the window grilles and boundary wall mentioned above, are more or less standard features in Colombo houses. In addition, all windows and doors should have good locks bolted from the inside. It is best to keep things locked whenever you can to eliminate temptation from both within and without, though with a degree of common sense about keeping valuables away from where stray hands can find them, your property should be reasonably safe.

Keeping Safe

Apart from basic security precautions, some people go so far as to provide themselves with 24-hour security guards for their homes—a mixed blessing perhaps as these men are usually not highly trained and not equipped to deal with a persistent intruder. Their biggest value comes from their constant presence and (hopefully) watchfulness which leave no opportunity for the casual thief. One side benefit: most of them keep a detailed log book with details of all comings and goings, so if you can't remember what time you came home the night before (or with whom!), there is always a way of checking up!

Dogs are useful additions, again for their presence rather than for anything that they might do to repel an intrusion. Many people keep dogs—sometimes very fierce ones— for this purpose, and even though they are primarily pets, they also serve a useful purpose as a convenient early warning system. Sophisticated alarm systems are available on sale and can easily be installed in your home.

THE SERVANT QUESTION

Nearly everyone faces the dilemma shortly after they have arrived of whether or not to hire domestic help. Doing so is fairly widespread in Sri Lanka, and it is a rare expatriate household indeed that does not have at least one servant in it. What kind of servant you should have, how many you should have and what you should pay them have of course to be determined by the individual concerned, but the following guidelines might be useful.

Many households have one servant (often male) who is the senior full-time servant and does a number of the main jobs in the house, including cooking and cleaning. It is he who takes the messages and who is in closest contact with the occupants of the house. It is also he who has the run of the house when the occupants are not at home, so it is therefore also important that he be perfectly honest.

Many such servants live in the house permanently and so it becomes as much their home as yours, along with all that this entails. Most Sri Lankan families like to employ live-in servants, so that the house is never left unattended, but some expatriates find the constant presence of outsiders in their home psychologically disturbing, and so prefer to employ some servants on a daily basis. In a number of cases, particularly in bachelor households, the house servant is the only one within the house and so does everything including such jobs as laundry and washing up. In larger households, it is also quite common to employ a second servant (often female) to help him out. She may take over the cooking, or the washing and ironing, or the cleaning or any combination of these and other tasks, but the end result is that some of the onus for doing everything properly is taken off the one servant.

The cook/maid can be a full-time or part-time employee depending on the need (and sometimes on how much you pay your houseboy in the first place). Other servants in the domestic ménage may include a driver (for those who fear to do daily battle with Colombo's awesome traffic) and/or a gardener/odd job man whose function it is to do anything that needs doing and which does not fall within the purview of the other servants!

Payment for the services of domestic servants varies considerably, but is still very low by Western standards. At the time of updating, a salary of Rs 10,000–12,000 a month for a full-time live-in servant is considered to be quite a good one, while a part time domestic would be satisfied with anything up to Rs 500–750 a day. Wages keep increasing though with the cost of living. A chauffeur is paid around Rs 18,000–20,000.

Hiring

How to hire a servant is a tricky question, and there are lots of possible answers. The most basic advice is never to hire a total stranger who appears out of the blue, or who isn't introduced to you by someone you know.

When the news spreads that you have newly arrived in Colombo, a succession of hopefuls looking for jobs will turn up at your door. All of them will have impeccable references if you examine them and probably 99 per cent of them are good, honest, hardworking people. The problem is the 1 per cent who are not, and how best to avoid taking them on by mistake.

This is where the advice and assistance of others who have been in Colombo for some while comes in useful.

Most domestic servants working in expatriate households have worked for foreigners before and have experience with their ways and preferences. As a result, there is a fairly extensive network among them, and it is usually well known on the grapevine when one of them is currently unemployed, because his previous employers have left. Thus, the servant of someone to whom you have been introduced will almost always know someone who is looking for a job, and who can be relied on to be fairly trustworthy, if so recommended. The recommender cannot afford to suggest for employment those who might not be trustworthy, as a tremendous loss of face is involved should problems occur. You are therefore probably quite safe to accept for employment—without too much checking—a servant who comes to you through this grapevine rather than off the street.

There are methods of checking if you wish to be scrupulous, such as asking to see the servant's registration book (though not all of the good ones have one by any means) or by checking with the local police. Doing the latter may not be strictly necessary if you are satisfied that you have a good and reliable worker, and may even get you off on the wrong foot. It is, however, worthwhile checking on the standard of cleanliness that is being maintained in your kitchen—though again there shouldn't be much trouble if you have made a good choice of employee.

On the whole, the question of servants is very much a matter of individual choice, but it is important to bear in mind that domestic service is not considered a demeaning profession in Sri Lanka, and that a well-treated servant is a valuable asset in a house for many reasons from cleanliness to security. Many of those who work in this profession will take pride in what they do and, if well treated themselves, will serve you well and loyally. They become almost family in their affection and loyalty.

MEDICINE AND HOSPITALS

Sri Lanka has two types of hospitals and two types of medical system which co-exist quite happily side by side. One is the traditional Western medical structure of general practitioners, specialists and hospitals with operating theatres and emergency units, and the other is the traditional practice of Ayurveda (or herbal) medicine, which predates the arrival of Western medicine in Sri Lanka by a good many centuries!

Western medicine is practised widely in urban areas and there is a comprehensive network of hospitals in these centres. General practitioners are not hard to find, the majority of whom are Sri Lankan trained, and generally as well up-to-date with trends in family medicine as their Western counterparts. Some of them may have done at least part of their training in Western countries.

There is a state sponsored medical scheme, but few specialists work exclusively in it, many of them being allowed to maintain private clinics as well

In Colombo, and one or two other larger centres such as Kandy, there are specialists, usually Western-qualified, available for consultation in all branches of medicine; the only speciality in short supply being psychiatrists.

for those who prefer to pay for privileged treatment. Similarly, hospitals are both public and private, the public ones usually being overcrowded and understaffed.

Expatriates living in Sri Lanka may make their own choice of doctor and determine the level of service they receive by what they—or whatever medical schemes they or their companies subscribe to—are willing to pay. On the whole, the standard of Western medical care in Sri Lanka is good; the equipment and techniques are not always the most modern but the expertise seems to measure up quite well to that in other parts of the world. Some private hospitals employ Indian medical personnel. Home nursing is available through a company named Ceylinco.

Staying Healthy in Sri Lanka

For a developing country, Sri Lanka has a well-developed health system which is available throughout the country. A 91.4 per cent level of literacy makes health education and family planning that much easier. The country has a crude birth rate of 18.4 per thousand, a crude death rate of 6.1 per thousand, and an infant mortality of 13.3 per thousand. Life expectancy averages 73 years.

Ayurvedic Medicine

This is a completely different experience. Many Sri Lankans still maintain that the natural remedies recommended by Ayurvedic physicians and used in Ayurvedic hospitals are far more effective than Western medicines, and in many cases, there is surprisingly substantial proof that this is indeed so. Balms and packeted Ayurvedic powders to be brewed are available in any grocery store or pharmacy. These are efficacious against the common cold or a touch of fever.

Herbs, potions and oils form the nucleus of what is used to cure everything from cancer to ingrown toenails, and some of the concoctions that are prescribed certainly smell and taste less than inviting. The *gulis* or Ayurvedic pills are sometimes hard to swallow because of their consistency or taste, and are therefore often administered with a coating of bees' honey. But they do seem to work, and those seeking a cure for a stubborn ailment that seems to be resistant to the wiles of Western medicine might be well advised to at least discuss the problem with those who have some knowledge of Ayurvedic cures. Conditions such as arthritis are found to respond well to oils and application of *paththus*—boiled or otherwise prepared poultices. Most hotels now have Ayurvedic centres, where an oil massage can be really good. Massage centres function in Colombo as units ranging from exclusive, exotic spas to less expensive centres, one of which is attached to an Ayurvedic hospital—the Siddhalepa medical centre in Dehiwala.

SHOPPING

Shopping in Sri Lanka generally falls into two categories: that which has to be done and that which one enjoys doing. The first includes such mundane chores as getting the groceries and repairing what is broken, while the second includes everything from clothing to handicrafts.

Grocery shopping covers both the daily marketing trips for perishable produce and the supermarket routine for the larger items. Many people have their servants do the former chores, keeping a book in which they record what they have spent, while they themselves perform the latter. If you want to do your own marketing, you should be aware that you might end up paying higher prices for most items than the locals do. Also be aware that prices are seasonal and depend to a large extent on where the produce comes from and how constant the supply is.

> Fruits and basic commodities always tend to go up in price during festival seasons, such as the April New Year and Christmas, because the demand is high, and there are large profits to be made.

Supermarket shopping is very similar to that in Western countries—fixed prices and cashiers at checkouts—but again the supply is not always constant. One week there may be a ketchup shortage and the next it could be cereal, depending on what ships have arrived in the port that week. On the whole, however, the supermarkets in Colombo are efficient and shortages are rare. The best thing about supermarkets is that they are open long hours and all day on Sundays.

More pleasurable shopping can also be done six days a week in most locations, particularly in both the government-sponsored and private handicraft shops. There are at least three big department store chains, and also the one for local produce, frequently having shops in the provincial towns—Laksala, a government-owned store in which it is possible to buy everything from table linen to teak, from brassware to batik. Prices are very reasonable in these shops and are stringently controlled, thus eliminating the (to some) rather tedious chore of bargaining for a fair price.

Clothing can also be had for a very reasonable price, with many large shops mainly in the Colpetty area offering quality export items—even winter clothes! Although there are no discount shops as such in Sri Lanka, many 'discount' items can be found, especially in the Maradana and Pettah areas of Colombo, where attractively made local garments, some designed originally solely for export, can be found on sale in many of the 'boutiques'.

COPING WITH CHILDREN

Expatriates in Sri Lanka usually send their children to one of the private schools which flourish in Colombo. Branches of one or two exist in Kandy. Lesser ones dot themselves all over the country. The local system is good but overcrowded, and most of the lessons are conducted in Sinhala or Tamil, which deters even the hardiest of cross-cultural aspirants. Recently, many large government schools in Colombo have started 'English streams' where the medium of instruction in classes is English. The foreign private (or 'international') school curriculum is usually modelled on the American or the British system, the schools catering mainly for those in the expatriate community and Sri Lankans who wish to prepare for post-secondary education abroad.

Out of school, children spend much of their time in self-directed activities, as there is little organised for them outside the schools which they attend. For teenagers, there are Western-style discos in the major hotels, and younger children often take the kinds of extracurricular lessons traditional in the West—ballet for girls and sports for boys—but, as with adults, there is little mixing between expatriate and local children in these activities, the two substructures of children's activities co-existing quite independently of one another.

When parents go out at night, smaller children are usually looked after by servants. This is no problem even if the family lacks a stay-in domestic, provided arrangements are made in advance with the daily visiting servant, and that it has been made clear that this is one of the duties expected of the servant. Hiring an external babysitter is not a common practice and best avoided unless you know the person who is going to be responsible for your children.

NIGHTLIFE

Neither Colombo, nor anywhere else in Sri Lanka for that matter, is a hotbed of nightlife. Sri Lankans are by and large an early to bed, early to rise people, whose social life revolves around the home rather than around the nightclub.

Of course there are nightclubs, particularly in Colombo, and they are well patronised, along with the discos that the major hotel chains seem to consider indispensable. These, however, along with the clubs mentioned in an earlier section, are mainly patronised by expatriates and wealthy Westernised Sri Lankans, rather than by the man in the street. The nightclubs are of the 'flashy' Western variety and provide very good entertainment—for a price. Discos are mainly for the young crowd and are currently very popular, but offer nothing culturally to distinguish them from their look-alikes in any other part of the world.

An added attraction are the casinos with the usual promotional gimmicks: free drinks, lavish buffets and even initial free stakes. Most of them advertise that they are exclusively for expatriates, but the locals, when recognised, are made welcome. Big spenders could have Mafia-like connections to drug smuggling and currency rackets.

Less respectable pleasures are also available in Sri Lanka. Sex is for sale if you want to look for it, but it is not obtrusive in the way

> The government clamped down on casinos and gambling due to religious pressure mostly, but with the opening up of the economy to market forces in 1977 and influx of foreigners, they came into existence again.

it is in some other Asian cities. In fact, there is comparatively little of a subculture in Colombo.

CLUBS

One of the many decisions faced by the newly arrived expatriate is whether to join one of the many clubs that proliferate in the Colombo area especially, or whether to remain an independent entity, not clearly identified with any one specific interest group.

Although all the clubs in Sri Lanka are now open to both Sri Lankans and expatriates in theory, in practice the two groups tend to be mutually exclusive by choice. There are few Sri Lankan members at the Colombo Swimming Club, for instance, as it has long been regarded a traditional expatriate watering hole, while a white face at the Otter Swimming Club not that far away is still a bit unusual. The Yacht Club, the Golf Club and the Hill Club in Nuwara Eliya all manifest this dichotomy to a greater or lesser degree, though it is now quite clearly a self-imposed restriction.

Unfortunately, too, in terms of mixing with the locals, all the clubs are also largely, by their very nature and by virtue of their large entrance fees, peopled by wealthy Sri Lankans rather than by members of the population at large. 'Clubbing' together is, in fact, a Western phenomenon, introduced into Sri Lanka by the British, and not a traditional practice among the majority of the population. This may well have its advantages for some, but it should not be forgotten that the local people to be encountered at the various clubs are atypical of the Sri Lankans as a whole.

There are other experiences in which people join together— balls at the big hotels being one of the most popular—but again the same rule applies: either it is usually exclusively one national group or another who participate, or else it is mainly a meeting between Westerners and those who would like to be Westerners if it were not for the colour of their skins!

CINEMA AND THE THEATRE

Good quality films are not screened regularly enough in the cinemas in Colombo and elsewhere, but a few cinemas do screen Hollywood and British productions such as some Oscar winners a couple of months later. Film festivals are held by the cultural units of some embassies: French, German, Italian. The American Centre in Colombo 2 and the Indian Cultural Centre in Colombo 4 have film screenings, once a week in the former centre and twice monthly in the latter. The International Centre for Ethnic Studies in Colombo 8 and the Russian Centre in Colombo 7 have once a month screenings. The ICES concentrates on avant-garde, mostly European and Asian films while the Russian Centre screens popular vintage Hollywood and other films. The English theatre is alive and sporadically stages plays, usually comedies. Two symphony orchestras and smaller musical groups cater to the music lover. Video and DVD rental stores are aplenty.

LIFE ON THE STREET

Dealing with beggars is something that comes naturally to people who have always been used to their presence, but it is a practice that is hard to learn at first. There are so many beggars in Sri Lanka that it would be a practical impossibility to give something to all of them, and a rule must be formulated to help the expatriate in continual confrontation with the begging fraternity.

The problem is that only some beggars are genuine hardship cases. There can be no doubt that, especially in the aftermath of so much social upheaval in the country, there

Beggars often line the streets of Sri Lanka.

are many dispossessed people who must make their living by begging. Oddly enough, it is these beggars who are usually passive: they sit and watch you go by and it is easy to feel compassion for them.

The aggressive ones—many congregate outside supermarkets and other places frequented by expatriates— are rumoured to be part of a syndicate controlled by a shadowy Mr X who brings them to their pitches every morning and collects them in the evening, charging them a part of their take for the privilege of doing so!

Everybody who lives in Sri Lanka for a while develops some strategy for dealing with beggars—giving to some and not to others, or not giving to any at all. Most tend not to give to the 'whining' beggars, whose approaches antagonise the potential donor; the pathetic beggars are luckier with their less abrasive approach.

Beggars are a fact of life in Sri Lanka. Learn to deal with them in a way that minimises annoyance and maximises the feeling that, by giving, a contribution has been made to a cause that is worthwhile. Some Sri Lankans, especially Buddhists, consider that giving to beggars helps them acquire merit—in the same way that their donations to the temple do—and will even go so far as to seek out local destitutes to whom to distribute leftovers from dinner parties. Some sort of similar frame of mind might also help the expatriate to decide whether or not to follow conscience or instinct.

CHARITIES, CONS AND RIP-OFFS

For foreigners who wish to give some of what they earn to worthy causes, Sri Lanka presents a dilemma: it is very difficult to differentiate between the legitimate and the bogus.

From the time that the newcomer moves into his house, there will be a never-ending stream of visitors at his door asking for money. All will come armed with official-looking papers proving their authority to collect for this or for that charity, and some of them are no doubt genuine, but a far larger number are completely fictitious.

There is no easy way to distinguish the true from the false, but if you are attracted by the cause and wish to test

Dane, almsgiving to monks, is a widely practised and 'safe' means of giving.

its authenticity, or that of its purported representative, there is one useful way to do it. Offer the caller a donation in the form of a cheque—no cash—made out to the organisation he purports to represent. If it is accepted, both the caller and the charity are probably genuine; at least they will have a bank account. The chances are that the caller will decline your offer, and after a last attempt to persuade you to part with cash instead, will probably leave. Given the circumstances, it is unlikely that you will see him again at your door!

There is one other practical way to safeguard yourself against giving money to con men under false pretences. If you can check out that the place or organisation that the man purports to represent actually exists, you can usually assure yourself that you are not giving money under false pretences. The best way to do this is by going there, but if you can't do this, the request to make a phone call to the institution or the intention to enquire from the police will often sort out the sheep from the goats.

The simplest way to deal with this question of giving to charity is to make a personal policy of giving nothing at the door, assuaging your conscience, if you wish, by donating regularly through one of the local churches or temples, or directly to a charity that you know to be legitimate. There are plenty of people who could use genuine donations in Sri

Lanka; it is a shame to waste this money on those who wish to take it from you under false pretences!

Other forms of con men—the touts and spurious guides—are easier to spot and, although some of them can be persistent, easier to get rid of. These operators play on the Western mentality and conscience, offering 'cheap deals' and over-helpfulness. The old adage, *caveat emptor* (buyer beware), is again the best advice when dealing with people whose credentials you are not sure of—in the long run, you will get exactly what you pay for.

GETTING AROUND

*'When they travel together a great many of them,
the Roads are so narrow that but one can go abreast
... and so they go talking along together,
and everyone carrieth his own provisions
on his back for the whole journey'*
—Robert Knox

Moving around has always been an integral part of life in Sri Lanka. At first on foot and then on horseback, in carts and carriages, Sri Lankans have always been able to travel the length and breadth of the country—owing to its small size—regardless of where they live. The northern peninsula was sporadically closed to visitors due to the LTTE conflict. The A9 highway was opened during the 2001–2004 ceasefire, with traffic and people being moved to and from Jaffna but having to undergo severe security checks both by government officials and the LTTE. With the defeat of the LTTE in May 2009, the A9 was opened again, ensuring safe passage as before the conflict. A domestic airline continues airlifting civilians from 2000, once Jaffna was liberated from LTTE control. Air service is available to Jaffna and to one or two other major cities from Ratmalana airport—close to Colombo. An air service now links some of the major cities.

Nowadays, because of the extensive system of villages in the country, and the need for efficient and low cost transportation systems between them and the urban centres, an island-wide train and bus network has become a necessity to ensure that people are able to move around freely and more or less when they want to. However, travelling about is not always as easy as it should be.

Sri Lanka poses a number of unique hazards for the traveller, and it is always best to consider the most efficient means of transportation before setting out on any journey. What is the most efficient means to get to one destination is not always the most efficient way to reach another, and it is usually best to weigh the available alternatives carefully before setting out!

Transport Costs

Public transportation in Sri Lanka is remarkably cheap. In cities, the bus fare is usually Rs 4 minimum, though it increases the further the distance travelled. For longer journeys, tickets are still a bargain: for instance, the intercity train between Kandy and Colombo, non-stop (120 km) and an efficient way of making the journey, costs Rs 220 each way and Rs 400 (2009 prices) if you opt for a seat in the Observation Car. Other journeys, including the much longer trips between Colombo and Jaffna, are similarly good value. No train runs to Jaffna, it stops short beyond Anuradhapura.

The CGR (Ceylon Government Railway) has been running at a loss, hence facilities are not up to standard. However, a overhaul is planned. Air-conditioned intercity express buses ply between most important cities. The fare to Kandy from Colombo is Rs 200. Private transportation by car is also of quite good value—an air-conditioned taxi costs Rs 60 per metre. This is the price quoted by a well-patronised company, ACE Cabs. They run an airport taxi service at Rs 1,250 for dropping a person at Katunayake, and a trip both ways costs Rs 1,650 plus Rs 100 for parking charges (April 2009 prices). Vans too can be hired. Many such taxi services are available in Colombo, but less so in Kandy and Galle. Three-wheelers, not metered as a rule (and drivers don't use them if they are!), will get you to your destination even more cheaply, but you'll have to be prepared to bargain for the price before you step in!

Cars and Driving

For the uninitiated, driving in Sri Lanka is a frightening experience. Rules exist, but they are haphazardly obeyed, and only sometimes enforced. The only one understood is 'Give way to anything bigger than you are'. This is particularly true of buses and lorries (trucks) whose persistence in being first would be commendable if it were not at times so frightening!

In addition to the non-observance of rules, drivers also have to contend with some situations that many drivers from overseas may never have encountered before: cows (and other animals) lying immobile in the middle of the road; cyclists who decide to make turns at the last minute in front of oncoming traffic; and pedestrians who appear to be totally oblivious of other road users. Of course, driving is worst in the cities, where the traffic is very heavy and sometimes too heavy for the road space available. Between 7:30–9:00 in the morning and 4:30–6:00 in the evening, traffic is particularly horrendous in major cities like Colombo, and for the cautious driver, these are probably times to avoid being on the road if you don't have to be. At other times, the traffic

is manageable, but 'defensive driving' is really not a possible strategy as it means that you would make little progress. A certain degree of aggression is necessary when driving in the cities, just to keep up with the flow. Some expatriates have almost got to the point where they regard Sri Lankan city driving a sport, while others liken the whole situation to a giant dodgem circuit!

Outside the cities, the situation is not so bad, and in fact, driving on some roads can be almost a pleasure when the traffic is light. The most annoying problems when driving 'outstation' (a Sri Lankan expression) are the generally poor standard of road maintenance and the narrowness of the road in some places, especially through the centre of towns, due to the fact that Sri Lankan roads were never initially designed to handle the amount of traffic that now uses them daily. Both these problems are being addressed and some of the roads outstation are newly covered and smooth to drive on, but it will take time for them to come up to international standards. In the interim, motorists may have to put up with bottlenecks and some rutted road surfaces. The road to Nuwara Eliya through the Ramboda Pass is now excellent.

Getting hold of a car is not a difficult task in Sri Lanka. For the long-term resident, cars can be bought quite easily and there are a variety of sources to buy them from. Garages abound, both motor dealers and small repair shops, the former of which generally have cars for sale on their premises while the latter can usually obtain something to your specifications if asked and given a few days. Cars range from brand new and extremely expensive to reconditioned cars imported from Japan and sold at a reasonable price, to second-, third- (and more) hand cars bought on the open market from garages and/or individuals. The only real rule of thumb when buying a used car in Sri Lanka is the old adage *caveat emptor*. You may not always get what you pay for! There is no official control over the sale of used cars, nor is there any inspection required, so it is best when buying a car either to know something about what you are doing or to make sure that someone comes with you who does know.

The Bureaucracy of the Road

For those who wish to become motorised in Sri Lanka, there are several places with which to become acquainted:

- The Registrar of Motor Vehicles deals with all the bureaucratic paraphernalia of registration of ownership, licences and testing, but as it is always bulging with people, it is not usually possible to make a very speedy visit.

- The Automobile Association of Ceylon is quite helpful to foreigners who want to buy or hire a car. They provide a breakdown service in most parts of the country.

- Insurance companies are willing to provide motor vehicle facilities to newcomers; bring a letter from your last insurance company if you are seeking discounted rates. There's competition among companies, so services offered are good.

If you don't want to buy a car, hiring one is relatively easy. Self-drive cars are not really recommended as many of them tend to be in very dubious condition, and cars with drivers are readily available. In fact, for a family, it costs very little more to hire a car and driver for a journey than it does to take public transportation or to drive your own car. Many people who own cars do not like to drive them for long distances and prefer to hire a car and driver for holidays or weekend trips. There is usually a set rate per kilometre for the rental of the car and a subsistence allowance for the driver on top

Getting a driver's licence if you are a long-term resident isn't difficult either. An international driver's licence is valid if you are not going to stay more than 12 months and you need nothing else, but if you are going to stay longer than this—or if you wish to have one—a Sri Lankan licence can be purchased on production of your licence from your home country. Interestingly enough, Sri Lankan driving licences do not have expiry dates, so even after you leave, they could prove to be a very practical souvenir!

Taxis

One of the definitive experiences in Sri Lanka is to ride in a three-wheeled trishaw—familiarly known as a three-wheeler or *bajaj* (after their Indian makers) or a *beep beep* (because of the noise made by their continually sounding horns). They operate in all the cities in the island and can be hailed even in villages. Most times, setting the price is a matter of negotiation based on both the distance and the time that the driver estimates it is going to take him to get there. Like all drivers of hired vehicles the world over, the price first mentioned will be significantly higher than the price you should actually pay, so be prepared to bargain before you ride. You will usually know when you have reached an approximately fair price by the driver's reluctance to go any lower!

Bajajs have a character all their own when they are moving, and the way that they weave in and out of the traffic is usually alarming and sometimes quite disconcerting. Some people refuse to use them because of the vulnerability of the passengers, and it is true that you would have little protection in a collision, but the drivers are usually very skilful at manoeuvring their vehicles and it is rare that a *bajaj* actually comes to grief. The three-wheeler is a very popular mode of travel for the woman who does not favour

A *bajaj*, the ubiquitous three-wheeler. A trip in one is rather like dodgems, but one generally arrives safely, if a little shaken, at one's destination.

the hazzle of driving herself. Many frequent users have 'their man' contactable by hand phone.

If you prefer something sturdier than an overgrown motorbike, there are taxis of other sorts also for hire. In Colombo, the major hotels all have taxi fleets which can be hired from the front of the hotel and these taxis are usually air-conditioned and with meters that work. They are, of course, more expensive than other types of taxi, but are reliable and relatively cool to ride in. In Colombo, radio taxi services are available which are very efficient. A phone call will usually produce a cab at your door within a few minutes, and although not all of them are air-conditioned, they too are metered so that there is no need to argue over the fare. The price on the meter is paid at the destination and that is that. If the taxi is needed at a rush hour, it's best to book early. Airport taxi services from Colombo are proving very popular, and a tourist board supervised taxi service from the Katunayake international airport is preferred by many a traveller to having his driver or relative pick him up.

The Morris Minor

Time was when outside every railway and bus station, and in many other locations in major cities, you find fleets of incredibly ancient Morris Minor taxis, or Fords. These taxis did at one time have meters and some of them still do, usually on the outside of the front fender, but few of them work and once again reaching your destination for a reasonable price is a matter of negotiation.

The Morrises and Fords have been replaced by newer Japanese cars and, of course, the ubiquitous three-wheeler.

Trains, Buses, Boats and Planes

For those people who wish to travel a long distance and do not have a car nor access to one, there are all manners of public transportation available. Trains and buses go to all parts of the island with remarkable frequency and even the remotest village can usually be reached within a day by using a combination of transportation systems.

Trains leave Colombo from either the Fort Station or Maradana Station and go north, south and east. To the north, it is possible to go to the Culture Triangle area and slightly beyond, while going east will take you to Kandy and through the central hills to Badulla, sitting at the edge of the highlands. Another takes you to the east coast. South, the line extends to the cities of Galle and Matara where the line ends.

The long distance trains (to Badulla and Batticaloe) have second- and third-class carriages where prior booking of second-class seats is possible. All seats on the inter-city trains that run from Colombo to Galle and to Kandy can be paid for earlier. These trains have an observation car which equates itself to a first-class carriage. As of April 2009, a ticket on an inter-city train costs Rs 220 one-way and Rs 400 for a seat in the observation car. The observation car seats are invariably reserved.

A network of Intercity Express trains have reserved seats and these trains are comfortable and efficient. They cost a little more than the regular trains but the expense is well justified for the convenience of knowing that you have a seat and that there is a reasonable chance that your train will get to its destination on time!

Short distance trains have one seating arrangement—third-class. There is no system of reservations on these trains and when they are full as they usually are; people sit where they can—in the aisle, in the doorways and even in the toilets if there is no other place. This is actually not as uncomfortable as it sounds (except for sitting in a Sri Lankan train toilet which cannot be recommended) and sitting in the doorway can be a pleasant experience, as it guarantees the occupant a good breeze—something that is usually lacking in the interior of the carriages.

The most glamorous way to travel by train is on the Viceroy Special, which can be rented by private groups of over 30 members (maximum is 48), and although the cost is quite high to travel this way, it is a tremendous experience and one of the few remaining ways to be transported back to the days of the British in Ceylon. The train is hauled by one of the only four steam engines still in working condition in the island, and the coaches are the original first-class coaches of the now-superseded Ceylon Government Railway, cleverly refurbished to carry tourist passengers. To my knowledge, these coaches are the only genuine first-class coaches now running on the island, and they have one luxury that no other regular coach possesses—they are air-conditioned!

Bus transportation on the island is not as exotic as travelling by train—in any of its form—but it is cheap, frequent and convenient. In most of the major cities, there is a bus stop close to the railway station where buses to most of the outlying areas around that central location and to other cities on the island can be found.

Buses come in two varieties: government-owned (SLTB) and privately owned.

Government-owned buses are all fairly large (though their size varies depending on the size of the roads over which the bus has to travel). Some of them look rather dilapidated (as indeed some of them are) and it is quite possible that some of the seats will be broken or the lights not working. Two almost guaranteed circumstances are that the bus will be full and that the journey will be hot and tiring. But it will be cheap and it will get you where you want to go, in the process introducing you—by proximity if nothing else—to a side of Sri Lankan life that you might not otherwise see.

The private buses are usually smaller than the government buses—some of them are actually minibuses—and usually faster. In fact, they are sometimes too fast. The drivers have a reputation for being rather reckless at times as they are paid by the number of journeys they make in a day! The private buses run on the same routes that the SLTB buses do, but are usually air-conditioned and charge higher fares, so it is a matter of

This ferry on the east coast consists of a wooden raft poled across the river.

preference or availability which kind of service you use. Both kinds of bus have conductors to take the fares and both may leave you gasping for fresh air when you disembark!

Surprisingly enough, the abundance of water in Sri Lanka is not generally utilised for public transport. There are ferries at strategic locations on major roads where bridges have not been built (especially on the east coast road), some of which carry vehicles and some of which do not. There also used to be a ferry service from Mannar in the north to Rameswaram in the south of India, but this has been suspended for some time owing to the terrorist problem in the country. (There is often talk of re-opening it, but so far nothing has actually happened.)

Private boats can be hired in the fishing centres either to get from one place to another or for deep sea fishing, and it is also possible to rent boats for a nostalgic ride down the old Dutch canal that still connects Colombo with the port of Negombo to the north, or to meander along a river in certain southern towns like Bentota. But travel by water, pleasant though it may be, is not really a feasible way of seeing the country as a whole.

International airline services are good at Colombo's Bandaranaike International Airport, Katunayake, and most places in Europe, Asia and North America can be reached either directly or with only one connection. Internal flights to certain destinations like Jaffna and Galle are available, but it must be said though that flying is an expensive way of getting about this relatively small country and is only really to be recommended to those in a great hurry, or to those who are prepared to pay the considerable cost of an aerial look at the topography of the country.

Transport Hassles

Like any other public transport system in the world, problems do occur on Sri Lankan buses and trains. Watch out for pickpockets, often operating in gangs, and the occasional stray hand which is almost inevitable on buses as packed as they sometimes get in Sri Lanka. If something untoward happens, you will probably get little in the way of assistance from your fellow passengers, as in the current climate many people are afraid to speak up to a stranger who might be carrying a knife or a gun. However, the state-run enterprises are well organised to deal with mishaps and problems at the bureaucratic level. Stations have offices which will deal with complaints if necessary, while at bus depots you can nearly always find a sympathetic inspector. Private buses are the main obstacle: they are very haphazardly regulated and, although there is a Private Bus Operators Association, it is difficult to call much attention to a situation that has originated on a privately operated vehicle.

Riding a Bike

Many Sri Lankans ride bicycles—of both the motor and push variety—and it is quite a practical way to get around the island. Bike riding in Sri Lanka, however, is not without its hazards. Other traffic usually goes about its business somewhat oblivious of bicycles, and being forced off the road is not uncommon. Westerners also suffer from the delusion that bicycles—unless specially constructed—are only meant for one; two is common and up to five is possible on a bicycle (the law notwithstanding) in Sri Lanka!

Bicycles can easily be bought locally. Motorcycles are usually small Japanese varieties, though the 'hot rod' style

is gaining in popularity. Push bicycles are often the old-fashioned type and are reasonably cheap to purchase. All bicycles, of whatever type, must be licensed in Sri Lanka and the licence displayed on the machine itself. If buying a bicycle is not a practical proposition, they can usually be rented fairly easily in most of the major cities and tourist resorts, but should be inspected carefully prior to taking them on the road, as not all are in a particularly roadworthy condition.

In case of bike failure, there are a very large number of bicycle shops on the roadsides, all of which have at least one man who can affect on-the-spot repairs. It may be a patch-up job but it will get you going so you need have little fear of being stranded on a bike anywhere in Sri Lanka. Remember, though, that the central areas of the island are almost all hills, and that riding a bike here is mainly for the strong or for those people who have plenty of time in which to reach their destination! If you choose your starting location correctly and take the journey leisurely, riding a bike is a tremendous experience and can enable you to see much that would otherwise escape you.

Animal Power

'Elefacts'

Wherever you go in Sri Lanka and no matter how you get there, your chances of seeing an elephant at work or at play are high. Right on the main roads or even more frequently along the smaller ones, working elephants are still a common sight: lifting large trees, moving heavy objects or pressed into service as makeshift tow-trucks! Under the control of their *mahouts*, or trainers, they are docile and well-mannered beasts, whose utmost delight when the day's work is done is to immerse themselves as fully as possible in a river or *wewa* and allow themselves to be scrubbed from top to bottom by their devoted riders. Wild elephants can be seen too, in reserves, of course, and on the roads in the forest encircled north central provinces, but these beasts are not so predictable—it is wise to admire them from afar rather than try to make their acquaintance from close up. In herds, they are okay but a lone 'rogue elephant' has to be treated with great resepct. They have been known to chase cars reaching a speed of 30 mph! Travelling beyond Polonnaruwa to the east or north will invariably give you exciting views of herds grazing peacefully. In September, they gather in their hundreds near the Minneriya Tank close to Polonnaruwa. Approximately halfway on the Colombo-Kandy road is an orphanage for baby elephants at Pinnawela—one of the attractions in Sri Lanka that is a must for the animal lover!

Sri Lanka is renowned for its elephants and taking a ride on one is still possible—if a price can be agreed with the *mahout* and the distance is not too great. Now they are mainly used as working animals, and ridden only for spectacular *peraheras*.

It is possible to make journeys to some destinations in Sri Lanka by using animal-powered transportation, but this tends to be very regional and very slow. For instance, in some of the very rural areas, and in some of the more traditional ones, public transportation is still partially dependent on bullock power. Bullock carts serve as ancillary local buses or taxis in some centres and they can be used as such both cheaply and safely. They are not of course renowned for their speed, and are not to be recommended when reaching one's destination on time—especially if another, faster, method is also available. But it is usually picturesque and tranquil, and a good way of getting to meet the locals, especially if you speak Sinhala, of course.

Although they were at one time abundant in Sri Lanka, and a very well-used method of getting around, horses have all but disappeared from the scene. The mounted police in Colombo will use some fine animals, but other than that, they are hard to find in public view. In some of the tourist centres, especially Nuwara Eliya in the hill country, where thoroughbreds are imported and raced from time to time, it is possible to hire some rather pathetic looking specimens for short rides into the surrounding countryside.

CULTURE SHOCK IN SRI LANKA

'It was a very sad condition while we were all together, yet hitherto each other's company lessened our suffering, and was some comfort that we might console one another. But now it came to pass that we must be separated and placed asunder, one in a Village, where we could have none to confer withal or look upon.'
—Robert Knox

In the midst of the euphoria of having arrived for a prolonged stay in a new country, it is very important to prepare for the sizeable psychological changes that will have to take place before becoming accustomed to a new environment.

No careful approach to the possibility of travelling and/or living and working overseas would be complete without at least some consideration of the phenomenon of 'culture shock'. Unlike a disease, culture shock is not selective, and its onset is an inevitable part of moving from a known environment to an unknown one. Whether your travels take you to Sweden, Swaziland or Sri Lanka, coping with culture shock—to whatever extent it might smite you—is going to be part of the experience.

There are several reasons why 'culture shock' is inevitable, but, unfortunately, the advantages of being psychologically prepared for it are not always obvious until it has taken its toll!

Support systems that have always been taken for granted suddenly disappear and leave a void which is hard to fill in a new environment. Family members who have been used to having their own individual lives over and above that of the family often suddenly find those personal contacts and pastimes temporarily missing, with the result that family members are suddenly thrown on each other's company full time—not an easy adjustment in itself. New problems arise for which there are no easily identifiable solutions from experience. The physical environment puts stresses on a body unused to coping with it, and above all, subtle challenges created by a new culture with new rules and new priorities arise to threaten one's own set of values.

Culture Shock for the Wife

The lot of the expatriate wife in Sri Lanka is quite a complex one. Those who come for employment alongside their husbands are generally fortunate, since finding any kind of employment 'on spec' is very difficult, and fraught with a large number of bureaucratic complications.

For those who don't or can't work, there is not a great deal to do during the daytime, especially if there are servants in the house. Some wives register and take courses in areas such as computers (there are an abundance of computer schools in the major cities) but for those without the inclination to involve themselves intellectually, or who live outside the major centres and do not have access to these facilities, life tends to revolve around social activities. Many learn a new craft like ikebana (Japanese flower arrangement) or play golf. National communities organise get-togethers for wives, at which they may play bridge or mahjong, or take trips together to places of interest. Many women are active in their children's schools; parents' associations rely heavily on their involvement.

It is not easy being a non-working wife in a foreign setting anywhere, and Sri Lanka is no exception. It is good for the wife coming to live in the country for a period of time to think carefully, well in advance of coming, about how she will occupy her time in a manner that satisfies her.

The Four Phases of Culture Shock

Experts writing on culture shock have identified four distinct phases that anyone beginning to live abroad goes through. The length of each phase varies from individual to individual, but in general, each phase lasts longer than its predecessor. The four phases seem to be:

- Fascination

  An initial period of time when everything is new; there are seemingly few problems since everyone is being extremely accommodating and the predominant feeling is one of

exhilaration at being at last overseas after a long period of anticipation.

- Friendship

  Immediately following the initial euphoria comes the stage in which the need to build a new social structure to replace the one left behind becomes paramount. At this time, there is an understandable but potentially dangerous tendency to gravitate exclusively to the company of one's fellow expatriates for friendship, and to take refuge in the familiar—a situation which can easily solidify into the 'we-they' syndrome in the third stage.

- Frustration

  After enough time has elapsed to become familiar with the country, to make initial contacts with the people and to come to grips with the requirements of the new job, a stage of depression begins (often inadvertently fuelled by the mutual support from the expatriate group), where the problems and difficulties that are inevitably part of the adjustment process seem to outweigh any possible, or potential, sense of achievement. The people seem to become intransigent, the physical environment unpleasant and the demands of the job impossible to fulfil, with the result that hostility towards the host country and those who are in authority in it becomes the predominant emotion, and homesickness results—sometimes to such a degree that there is a tendency (to which some people occasionally succumb) to decide that the whole experience is not worth it and that an early return home is preferable to remaining permanently miserable.

- Fulfilment

  Fortunately, although the previous stage can be a very difficult one to live through, it does usually come to an end with the growth of cultural awareness, and leads to a period in which the experience of being overseas becomes both fulfilling and rewarding. The onset of this phase stems from a personal realisation and acceptance that the new environment, in all its aspects, is unlikely to change, so that if the experience is to be satisfying, it is the individual who must adapt himself to his new environment by learning to operate within its confines. This may indeed result in compromises—often many of them—but it will also result in a realisation that conflicts can be worked out and that the potential for success and happiness during the time to be spent abroad is as great as the individual is prepared to let it be.

Anyone coming to live in Sri Lanka for an extended period of time is going to experience all of these emotions, hopefully including the final one, as Sri Lanka is not what it initially appears to be.

On the surface, an eastern country with a strong Western overlay, many things in Sri Lanka appear at first glance to be familiar or, at least, to work in familiar ways. Unfortunately, this often proves to be only a surface impression and it gradually dawns on the newcomers that this is so. The real Sri Lanka, in terms of its social and power structures and of its traditions, is a very un-Western one (as has been mentioned several times earlier in this book) and one moreover that may not be nearly as attractive or easy to understand on a closer look as it appeared to be on first acquaintance.

This is not to say that a Westerner, or for that matter any foreigner, coming to live in Sri Lanka cannot adapt to the country; it is easily possible to do so, and it is after all the purpose of this book to help you. But it is important to identify each phase of the culture shock process carefully as it occurs, and to be accepting of ways of doing things that may seem strange or even wrong to Western eyes. Not everyone likes living in Sri Lanka, and there are special stresses and strains put on those who are here by both the political and physical climate. There are, however, some practical ways of adapting and of enjoying the experience of becoming in small measure a part of the Sri Lankan mosaic.

Coping with the Trauma

Coping with 'culture shock' is a common part of the overseas experience and, as such, its symptoms need to be shared rather than suffered in silence.

Reactions to the manifestations of 'culture shock' should certainly be discussed with members of your family who have accompanied you overseas, and, if possible, in frank and honest discussions with your friends and colleagues who can often be of immense help. If neither of these avenues is possible, recording one's experiences in a journal and writing letters are also very therapeutic. Remember to tell friends and relatives to send you email regularly, and not necessarily to wait for your reply before answering. Receiving letters, email, SMSes and telephone calls can be very reassuring, and allow you to get on with establishing your daily routine with minimum worries. Apart from Skype, telephone calls taken in Sri Lanka on pre-paid cards are much cheaper than those that are overseas originated.

There is no way of avoiding culture shock when going to live in any new country, but there are ways to minimise its impact and to cut down on the length of time occupied by the frustration and hostility stage.

The first of these ways is to be aware of what is happening; to recognise the symptoms of culture shock and to share the feelings which each phase generates with others, so as to avoid the feeling of isolation which is so destructive in the long run. The second is to find new ways of coping with old (and new) problems, so that flexible thinking can lead to satisfactory resolution instead of permanent inertia. Finally, and perhaps most important, it is imperative to determine reasonable and achievable goals for the experience of living wherever you are (even if these goals have to be modified from those you hoped to achieve before you left home), and to find ways of reaching these goals, whether they be as simple as survival or as complex as cultural and linguistic understanding.

Above all, to succeed in the Sri Lankan culture, learn to participate in it and to integrate it with your own in as satisfactory a way as possible. Learning the national languages, Sinhala or Tamil, or both, at least to converse in, and understanding the local cultural traditions that permeate everyday life is a good way to start, and one that can accelerate substantially the gradual decrease of the impact of culture shock.

Co-existence or Integration?

For those people who find living in Sri Lanka hard, and there are many who do, the question arises whether it is better to suffer in silence and depart as soon as possible or whether there is any accommodation that can be reached to at least make the Sri Lankan experience tolerable, if not pleasant.

No one can develop personally without a culture, and the success of any overseas experience ultimately depends neither on how well you retain your own cultural behaviour in the face of opposition, nor on surrendering them completely, but on integrating the best aspect of your own social and cultural 'baggage' with that of the indigenous culture so that you can feel as equally at home in your new environment as you did in the one from which you came, and so open up for discovery a whole new world of possibilities.

For some, the answer to this means living entirely in the expatriate world—a quite possible, though expensive and somewhat narrow scenario, for those living in Colombo at least. For others who may not wish to go this far, it means a tacit tolerance of the facets of Sri Lankan life that cannot be avoided, often accompanied by a good deal of rather vituperative criticism in private among Western friends.

It is theoretically possible to live in Sri Lanka for a year or two like this, but such a lifestyle would be very sterile: co-existence at best and certainly not integration.

It may never be possible for most Westerners and other expatriates to become integrated into Sri Lankan society that they are indistinguishable from the Sri Lankans themselves in thought and deed—though you do meet the occasional Westerner who has been here for 10–20 years and has accomplished that. There are even some rare souls who are totally at home in the company of both expatriates and Sri Lankans, but for the majority, integration is going to be a limited experience at best. It is one worth striving for, however, as Sri Lankans individually are some of the most hospitable and friendly people you could hope to meet. Even limited integration into the society brings with it an insight into the lives of the people and their culture that is the ultimate purpose of anybody who has actively sought the experience of living and becoming part of another culture.

A VERITABLE FOOD FAIR

CHAPTER 6

'The main substance with which they fill their
bellies is Rice, and other things are but to give it relish ...
The great ones have always five or six sorts of food at
one meal, and of them not above one or two at most of
flesh and fish ... And after one is used to that kind
of fare, as they dress it, it is very savoury and good.'
—Robert Knox

THE FLAVOURS OF SRI LANKA

Since the days of Robert Knox's captivity, the island has progressed from bullock cart to luxury limousine; from conveying letters and poetic messages through the air by special carrier birds to satellite and electronic communication. Yet it retains its basic food habits, not only from the era of Robert Knox, but even from the time the country was dubbed the 'Granary of the East' in the 12th century AD. Flavours and variations have been added and influences introduced along the way as Dravidian invasions from the south of India swept across the land; as Arab traders voyaged to Ceylon and married and settled down; and as the Portuguese, Dutch and English arrived as bargainers in the spice trade and soon turned into exploiters and colonisers.

RICE AND CURRY

Rice and curry is *the* food of Sri Lanka. However, in the last century, following the example of the tea-planting European community, brown *sahibs* and indigenous wealthy weight-watchers, the term should logically be switched to read curry and rice.

Rice and curry, curry and rice, whichever is the predominant component, makes for a balanced meal.

Typically, rice—fluffy white or nutritionally brown from raw cereal or even parboiled—is served with a number of curries, cooked, fried, simmered and raw. When festivity demands, rice is cooked in coconut milk (juice extracted by squeezing scraped coconut kernel) and saffroned slightly to give it an eye-catching hue or fried in *ghee* (butter from cow's milk) to make *buriyani* (biryani as the Indians and Pakistanis say) with chunks of mutton or chicken. Savoury rice is tossed with sauteed vegetable, meat pieces and scrambled egg. Curry leaves, cardamom, a stick of cinnamon, and crushed ginger with grated garlic produce an aromatic steam in the piled up rice that has the nose and salivary glands working overtime.

Curries are varied but usually one has a meat and/or a fish dish, a pulse (dhall, greengram, chickpeas), two vegetable dishes and a *mallung* (certain kinds of green leaves shredded fine and lightly cooked with chopped onion and green chilli, often with a fistful of coconut stirred in). A raw salad is a frequent accompaniment. In these lie the necessary starch, protein, fats and oil, vitamins, minerals and salts for a balanced diet.

Resthouses and Sinhala restaurants never ever serve a rice and curry meal without the *pol sambol* and crisp, big-bellied fried *papadam*, an excellent counterpoint to fiery curries. *Pol sambol* is ubiquitous, made as it is by lightly pounding or grinding scraped or desiccated coconut, dried chilli, salt, onion and Maldive fish. Take away the coconut and one has the ever so popular *lunu miris* or *katta sambal*—dynamite to the foreigner but essential to the local palate.

'To give it a relish' as Knox says, typical meals carry an assortment of 'rice pullers'— chutneys, pickles and *baduns*, the latter being *karola badun* (fried dried fish), often admittedly strong smelling, or dried sprats or prawns.

BRING ME THE FIRE EXTINGUISHER, PLEASE

This brings up the matter of chilli. Yes, Sri Lankan food is very spicy and very hot—chilli hot. Green peppers are much used, powdered or ground-blazing hot red chilli is incorporated and black pepper is often added, catalysing the explosive effect. The uninitiated takes a bite and feels as if fire is consuming him or red ants in hordes are nipping his tongue.

The best practical cure for this is to sip very warm water—the hotter the better. Stars are seen, tears gush forth, the nostril sluice gates open wide, but the feeling of being on fire disappears rapidly. The wisest preventive, of course, is caution. Take sips and nips or play safe and pass on the hot dishes. Stick to white curry, *mallung* and *papadam*. In practice, however, all this might be unnecessary, as your Sri Lankan hostess will be very concerned about your delicate foreign palate and bland-trained taste buds; hotel chefs are equally concerned. So go ahead and eat your watered down curry and rice, but get acclimatised to chilli eventually, or else you will miss out on a true Sri Lankan taste experience.

THE STAFF OF LIFE

Time was when in traditional extended family homes, four meals of rice were the order of the day. Yogurt was eaten with rice accompanied by the ubiquitous *pol sambol*. Bread was a rarity then, unlike today, when even the poorest prefer the convenience of a run to the closest shop for a loaf or loaves to the bother of cooking a meal.

The elite of the land start the day with a continental or English breakfast, have curry and rice for lunch and dine in Western style. Hence the traditional divisions between the kitchen staff in wealthy homes. The *kussi amma*—buxom, kindly and female—is an expert at rice and curry and can turn out preparations of rice flour that often go to make the evening meal or breakfast. The higher paid *cook appu*—male invariably—boasts of his ability to make *istubeestake* and *cutlis* (the Sri Lankan English rendering of the more familiar Western terms) for the foreign palate.

Sinhalese breakfast foods include *kiribath*, rice cooked in thick coconut milk, gooey and delicious, cut into squares or diamond shapes and eaten with *pol sambol* or *katta sambol* or *jaggery*. Breakfast could also be of *stringhoppers*, made by squeezing a mix of rice flour or wheat flour and water through a wooden mould with a finely perforated base, on to circular rattan or plastic mats. These are piled in a steamer and, when correctly steamed, emerge light and delectable. *Stringhoppers* broken up and tossed in margarine with vegetables become *pillau*—a good alternative to yellow rice.

Hoppers will delight you: crisp at the edges, soft and pancakey in the centre. You could eat *hoppers* with butter, jam or grated *jaggery* or with a watered down chicken or beef curry, while your Sri Lankan host will have his with *seeni sambol*, made of finely sliced onion cooked in oil with plenty of Maldive fish and chilli powder—and the never absent

A breakfast consisting of curry, *hoppers*, *stringhoppers*, *sambols*, gravy and bananas.

katta sambol. Roti is like unleavened bread; *pittu* comes in cylindrical or conical mounds according to the utensils used for steaming the dexterously produced fine-grained mix of rice flour, scraped coconut and a dash of water.

Congee—rice boiled with a good quantity of water, to which is added a squeeze of thick coconut milk and ground or liquidised green leaves of particular varieties—makes for a healthy breakfast porridge.

Rice is also the staple of Sri Lankan Tamils, but eating with your Tamil friends would be easier on your palate. Chilli is used less, there is more gravy in the form of *rasam* (pepper water) and delicious *sambar*, a curry of several vegetables and dhall cooked together. A favourite dinner would be of *thosai* made of *ulundu* flour and of *vade*. For breakfast, you may be served *ittli*, a small conical cake of flour and other ingredients steamed to compactness.

North Indian food served in many Colombo restaurants includes *naan* and *parata* eaten with curries which look strong but are very mild. A super pre-meal drink is *lassi*—liquidised yogurt, sweet or salted.

> Invited to a Muslim dinner, you will doubtless be served *buriyani* and often you will be called upon to tackle a roast chicken whole. A green pulverised mint *sambol* and a cashewnut and green pea curry will make for an easy-to-eat, un-hot meal. Dessert will be *vatalappan*—a delicious custard or caramel pudding, rich with *jaggery* and coconut milk and spiced with cardamom and nutmeg.

CUTLERY VERSUS FINGERS

Of course, a typical Sri Lankan meal should be eaten Sri Lankan style. Use your fingers. When mixing the rice with curry, take bits of this and pinches of that, lightly mix with a bit of rice with your finger tips and pop it in your mouth. Avoid getting your palm and fingers above the knuckle soiled. That is considered not quite polite.

If you don't like using your fingers, call for cutlery. This is usually provided, even at meals you are invited to in a home where only Sri Lankans are expected. But there is a reason why the locals prefer using their fingers when ready to enjoy a leisurely meal. Rice and curry wrapped in slightly 'toasted' plantain (banana) leaf has just a bit of an

In the past, left-handers were compelled to use their right hands for eating with, thus making them either ambidextrous or frustrated, but now it is perfectly all right to use the left hand, which long ago was usually reserved for another more basic purpose!

aromatic advantage over a meal dished out on china. It is the same with using one's fingers: the meal seems tastier. Muslims are reputed to eat off a common plate, or rather, tray, with no cutlery visible even to serve yourself curries! However, this practice is only prevalent at very custom-bound ceremonies such as a traditional Muslim wedding or a Ramadan festival lunch. You are excused if you indicate preference for using a plate and request fork and knife or spoon.

A note about religious beliefs as they impinge on food habits seems appropriate here. Buddhists have, as one of the five precepts they are advised to observe, to promise to refrain from taking life, which means not eating flesh, fowl and fish. Appetites and desires being what they are, though, Buddhists often circumvent this with the rejoinder 'But I did not ask for that bull/cow/goat/fowl to be slaughtered, nor for the fish to be caught.' There is, however, a greater awareness of the brutality involved, the value of each being's life, the ingratitude of consuming the flesh of the animal that nurtured your child with its milk and very significantly, the benefits of

vegetarianism. So you will find that many of your Buddhist friends are non-meat eaters. But they do serve meats, seafood and eggs at the table most of the time, though there are certain festival times, like the Buddhist Vesak, when this is never done. Hindus are very often strict vegetarians.

Muslims insist on *halal* meat, the flesh of animals slaughtered by an approved butcher so that blood is shed; hence the non-use of humane pellet killing in Sri Lanka generally. As a result, a Muslim acquaintance you take out to dinner may seem finicky, although a reassurance that the meat is *halal* from the service staff or your cook will usually overcome his or her concern.

Regarding taboos, there is nothing to be cautious about, except with Muslims. Do not mention pork, pigs, bacon and never, ever serve such food if you invite a Muslim to a meal in your home. You will be excused if you ask in a Muslim owned/run shop for bacon—but only once or twice. If you keep being scatter-brained or short on sensitivity, you are eventually bound to receive a couple of black looks, if not non-service and short shrift.

The Cost of Food

This can be divided fairly rigidly into two categories: locally produced food and imported food. The former is quite cheap—certainly by Western standards—and a wide range of meat, vegetable, fruits and manufactured products are usually available. The meat and vegetables are generally excellent, and are 'just like home', if not sometimes better, but be a little careful with the locally produced manufactured products. It's not that they are suspect; most of them are of a very high quality. They are not always what they seem—the tomato ketchup is always spiced, for example.

Imported foods are considerably more expensive, increasingly so in fact, but are readily available. Cereal will cost you well over Rs 200 per box while imported meats can run much higher.

Eating and drinking in Sri Lanka need not be that expensive: but, for economy's sake, it is best to try and achieve a blend between what you can make do with what is produced locally.

A FEAST FROM THE SEAS

Sri Lanka is rich in seafood, a natural resource found plentifully all round the island, but not fully exploited due to the high cost of boat mechanisation and inadequate freezing facilities for long voyaging craft. The outrigger canoe is still used for night fishing. During the inter-monsoonal period (September through April in the south-west), pinpoints of light bob all along the horizon. They are lanterns of fishing canoes. Men throw nets into the water and they are drawn in the next morning by a group of around 20 men and boys, who tug and pull the net ashore in unison, often chanting a song which starts with the words "*Hodi helei heleiya*".

A particularly Sri Lankan form of fishing is engaged in by the stilt fishermen of Galle and its environs. The men perch themselves on stakes driven into the coral reef, and cast their lines to wait patiently for the fish to bite.

Seer is a very tasty white fish, particularly when egg-and-bread-crumbed and deep-fried, served with potato chips or French fries. Large tuna is a 'blood' fish which is cooked to a delicious curry by the southerner in an earthenware vessel

Stilt fishermen off the southern coast.

over a slow fire with a brazier of coals as a cover. Sprats make wonderful eating when dipped in batter and deep-fried.

Shellfish abound; crab, lobster, prawn and shrimp are abundant in the lagoons that punctuate the coastline, but they are pricey both in the market and on hotel menus because of the large export trade in them which brings in precious foreign exchange. An interesting sight is the catching—by hand mostly—of crab and prawn by men who wade into the lagoon and dazzle the crustaceans with very strong lamps or ignited torches of coconut leaves.

SPICES

At the gardens along the trunk road to the hill capital of Kandy, packeted spices are available in plenty, as they are in many shops. Sri Lanka's central position in the spice trade of yore is historically recorded, and this little dot in the Indian Ocean still grows, trades and exports spices. The better known and spicier are *enesal* (cardamom), *kurundu* (cinnamon), *karambu* (cloves), *suduru* (fennel), *maduru* (cumin), *sadikka* (nutmeg), *kaha* (turmeric)—more a colourer than an aroma giver—*rampa* (pandan leaves), *sera* (lemon grass) and *karapincha* (curry leaves). Coriander, too, is ground and used in curries. Tamil cooking incorporates *tamarind*—the sour pulp of the legume that grows abundantly in the dry zone.

> A habit in Sri Lankan cooking is to 'temper' curries. A spot of oil is heated, preferably in an earthenware *chatti*, mustard seed is thrown in, resulting in minor explosions and eruptions. Curry leaves, ginger, and a piece of pandan leaf are introduced to the oil. Lastly, the cooked curry is added to the mixture.

Some of these condiments, toasted and ground, or pounded and added to curries, most definitely introduce an appetising smell and taste. This mixture is termed curry powder; the Sinhala name, *thunapaha*, when literally translated reads 'three five', probably a clue to the bare essentials that are needed to turn out a full-bodied curry powder.

SWEETMEATS

In Sri Lanka, one hardly talks of sweets or candy, because sweets to the local are sweetmeats! The different nationalities

Western Food

Just in case the true Westerner is experiencing complete panic about his taste buds, rest assured that cornflakes, cookies and children's food of the kind that comes in tins, packages and bottles can also be found easily in Sri Lanka. Colombo boasts several supermarkets which are well stocked with whatever you need—though there are occasional mysterious shortages of some items. Hotels too usually always have one restaurant, or a part of one, devoted to the more usual Western types of fare. In fact, The Guinness Book of Records award for the most hamburgers sold in one month was at one time held by a Colombo hotel!

have their own distinctive kinds of sweets and most are oil impregnated. *Kavun* is the commonest; it is to the Sinhalese what rich cake is to the Westerner. Each and every auspicious occasion and festival sees plates of *kavun* and *kiribath* (squares of milk rice) being passed around. *Kavun* is rice flour cakes deep-fried without a knob rising in its centre called the *konde*. If the knob is made, then the result is a *konde kavun*. A greengram and flour paste produces another variety of *kavun*. Large, folded *stringhoppers*, deep-fried and doodled over with melted sugar or thick treacle makes *aasmi*. *Kaludodol* is rich, heavy in the stomach but delicious, again oozing oil since the ingredients that go into its many hours of vigorous stirring over an open hearth are rice flour, coconut milk and *jaggery*.

A special delicacy of the Kandyans from the hill country is *unduvel*—deep-fried out-sqeezings from a cloth pouch filled with a mixture of rice flour and *undu* (a kind of cereal) into hot oil in loops and circles. The cooked configurations are dropped into a *chatti* of treacle (thickened syrup of the kitul palm) and left to soak for a minute or two so that treacle oozes into the tunnels of the spaghetti-like twisted coils. It is crisp outside and soft and mushy inside—altogether a delight.

Tamils have their own sweets. One, a favourite and more a savoury than a sweet, is *murukku*. It resembles the Kandyan *unduvel*, but does not undergo the treacle treatment and is smaller, crisp and yellow or ochre in colour.

Sweets of Indian origin such as *jalabi*, *muscat* and *gulab jamuna* are full of ghee and available in Indian restaurants and shops that call themselves Bombay Sweet House.

The Burghers have their *foguete* and *kokis* and the Muslims specialise in *vatalappan*.

FRUITS

Sri Lanka is paradisical in its offerings of fruit. To match its range of climates and vegetation, varying from the arid, near desert dry zone, through the lush temperate hill country to the undergrowth thick virgin tropical forests of the wet zone, Sri Lanka boasts an abundance of fruit.

When in Sri Lanka, push aside that caramel custard and ice cream that hotels show a penchant for serving, and ask for fresh fruit. They may serve fruit salad but the better bet is to go for the fruit whole, meaning instead of making do with a diced and sugared cupful, demand a plate of mangoes, bananas,or a slice or two of pineapple. Or better still, buy your own fruit and enjoy a much larger piece at a smaller price!

Varied, juicy and delicious, tangy, pure sweet, sourish, sharp, bland and creamy, are some of the flavours and textures fruits such as the pineapple, mango, papaya, mangosteen and durian have to offer.

Bananas come in various shapes, sizes and even colours. Have you seen the deep red ones? Pretty to look at, but not to be compared with the common man's sour plantain or the aristocratic *puvalu*, a bright yellow, fat variety. Mangoes too are varied, ranging from the very small, very sweet *beti amba* to the large *pol* variety. Mangoes from Jaffna are heavenly. The soil and salinity of ground water have a special effect on the taste of the northern mango. Papaya is good for your complexion and health; marvellous at breakfast. Beware the pineapple if you are prone to rashes, itches and allergies.

Mangosteen and rambutan are seasonal. Both appear on sale in mounds on the roadside in Cinnamon Gardens and Havelock town (Colombo 7 and 5) in July and August. Learn the art of applying pressure to the mangosteen to split cleanly the dark pulpy outer covering in order to reveal pure white pods embedded in the dark crimson inner lining of the fruit. There's not that much to get your teeth into in a mangosteen, and for that matter in a rambutan either, but the effort of getting to the flesh is worth it. The seedless rambutans, needless to say, are easier to eat but harder on the purse. The local tears open the skin of a rambutan with his teeth. This for sure is what causes sore throats, a common offshoot of eating too many of these fruits. Cut open the skin without endangering your health by biting into the dusty and perhaps dirty outer cover.

Try a durian and the ripe pods of a jackfruit. They both have rather strong aromas, and the durian, some would brutally say, stinks. Be that as it may, the taste of the fruit is something not to be missed. The skin is covered with sharp spines. It can be split into sections exposing large pods of creamy, flesh covered seeds. Eat the flesh and savour its sophisticated and delicate flavour, described variously. A tinge of garlic may be detected. Iced, the pungency is reduced and the firmness of the flesh increased.

Ripe jakfruit comes in two varieties—stick to *varakas* which yields a firmer pulp and may 'drip with honey'.

Avocados are seasonal, but available at a price throughout the year. Diced and tossed with chopped onion and green chilli in salad dressing or a teaspoon of vinegar, avocado turns out to be a fine salad accompaniment to meat or fish. As a dessert, avocado can be scrapped off its jacket and eaten with sugar, treacle or a pinch of salt, or mashed with grated *jaggery* and milk. It also makes a good face mask for skin crying out for soothing after a day of sun, sea water and sand.

ALTERNATIVES TO COKE

Squeezed or liquidised, fresh fruits also make wonderful drinks. There's no better quencher for a parched throat than a tall glass of lime and soda, tinkling with crushed ice—fresh lime, remember! Local oranges are available at a price, green jacketed and sourer than the imported variety. Also don't miss out on a *passiona*—the drink made from passion fruit, the yellow tennis-ball-sized fruits that yield dark hard seeds with a soft smear of pulp. Liquidised, one gets bits and pieces of black seed floating around, but squeezed, the juice alone is extracted. With plenty of sugar and a pinch of salt, it makes a good drink. An even better drink results when the passion fruit juice is mixed with liquidised pineapple, a squeeze of lime in a base of soda with tiny cubes of apple floating around.

Sri Lanka is famous for its ginger beer, the home-made variety being better than the bottled stuff sold by Elephant House and other producers of soft drinks.

Beli is another fruit that makes a very interesting drink. The tinned stuff is good but eating it is better and healthier if you are not put off by the gum and hundreds of seeds within. *Beli* is reputed to have medicinal properties—it will stop diarrhoea or induce less toilet tribulation.

Tambili beats any other drink, and is a nutritious thirst-quencher.

In the city or while travelling around, you can substitute coke, soda and bottled water with *tambili*—the water of the young orange coconut. *Kurumba*, the green young coconut, is also a healthful drink.

You could, while travelling, break your journey for a few minutes beside a *tamlibi* vendor. He will expertly render the nut into a drinkable form. If you desire the soft kernel within, he'll split the nut open and fashion you a spoon off the sliced husk. Don't worry, only the clean inside of the improvised spoon comes in contact with the kernel. Drinking straight from the fruit calls for dexterity and so you can use a straw instead. You can ask for a *tambili* even if you are dining in a hotel.

TWO LEAVES AND A BUD

Everybody knows that Sri Lanka's name is synonymous with good tea. Ceylon tea comes in two main varieties: high-grown and low-grown. This makes for a difference in strength. According to the process of manufacture, various flavours result, ranging from the subtle to the strong. Depending on the brand and kind (leaves, fannings, dust), the brew will differ in colour, aroma, flavour and taste.

If you accept a prepared cup of tea in Sri Lanka, expect your spoon to stand straight! The man on the street likes his 'cuppa' heavily sugared and milked.

The discerning, however, will opt for their own preparation. A slice of lime or a squeeze of lemon will make your tea a real refresher. Cold tea with lime is a pick-me-up for the teetotal traveller, parched and heat-fatigued. Ginger tea is superb, made by dropping a few pieces of pared fresh ginger in the teapot. There are five golden rules for making a good cup of tea:

- Use freshly drawn water
- Bring to the boil (do not use re-boiled water)
- Steam, or rinse the teapot with very hot water
- Add tea leaves to the still hot pot—one per person and one for the pot (you can reduce this if you need a lighter brew)
- Pour the boiling water in and let it stand for 5 minutes before pouring out the brewed tea

Tea can be bought 'loose' in packets or as tea bags. Green tea is available with different estate or brand names; so also flavoured tea like jasmine, vanilla, ginger and lemon.

Sri Lankans brew an assortment of other 'teas' from dried herbs, dried roots, even dried flowers. Sri Lankan coffee is strong; coffee leaves a sediment in the pot, cup and strainer. Health drinks are plentiful. Toasted coriander boiled with a few pips of garlic and slices of green ginger will most definitely help you get over a flu faster or prevent the sniffles. Steam of the brew inhaled loosens blocked sinuses.

DON'T DRINK THE WATER

Be sure you drink boiled water, if not boiled and filtered. If you still have qualms, stick to bottled water, preferably imported, beer, soda or better still *tambili*. The ice in your scotch may be straight off the tap and suspect, but the freezing and whisky will render it harmless.

Whatever you eat and drink, however, beware of being too cautious; for with food and drink, as with many other things in Sri Lanka, often the experience is well worth the risk!

ENJOYING SRI LANKA

'...they have their solemn and annual festivals.
Of these there are two sorts, some belonging to their
Gods that govern the earth, and all things referring to
this life; and some belonging to the Buddou. The greatest
solemnity is performed in the City of Cande; but at the
same time the like Festival or Perahar is observed in
divers other Cities and Towns of the land.'
—Robert Knox

SRI LANKAN FESTIVALS

Sri Lanka probably has more festival days than anywhere else in the world. At least once a month, and frequently more often, there is a public holiday when everything—or at least most things—close down and everyone has the day off. The current Sri Lanka calendar lists 29 public holidays for the year, more than any other country and only exceeded (according to Swissair's *Public Holidays Around the World*) by some parts of Australia!

The reason for this plethora of festivals and holidays is quite simple: Sri Lanka is a multi-ethnic and multi-religious community which observes all the religious holidays of its major faith (Buddhism) and the major festivals of the three remaining important faiths (Islam, Hinduism and Christianity).

In addition to religious festivals, there are also secular holidays such as National Day (February 4) and May Day, and even, from time to time, special holidays decreed by the government to commemorate some significant contemporary event. But just to modify the impact somewhat it seems, not all these holidays are days of rest for everyone: some of them are bank holidays when the banks are not open, and some are mercantile holidays when neither banks nor business are open, but the shops are!

Any foreigner coming to Sri Lanka soon learns to enjoy coping with the frequent holidays, made all the more enjoyable when they fall adjacent to a weekend and provide the opportunity to get away into the cool of the hills for a few days!

Poyas and Peraheras

The most common holiday in the Sri Lankan calendar is a Poya Day, which occurs approximately every 28 days. Poya Day is the day of the monthly full moon, a significant day for Buddhists as it marks the beginning of another lunar month. It is a day to go to the temple to hear *bana* preaching—sermons from the temple monks, or to listen to the chanting of *pirith*—the verbatim discourses of the Buddha in the Pali language. Many Buddhists take the day off to meditate and reflect on the teachings of Buddha by observing *sil*, the vow to follow the eight precepts as laid down by the Buddha.

For the non-Buddhist, Poya Day has become simply a regular public holiday, marked especially by the fact that no alcohol or red meat may be sold on that day, in deference to the Buddhist precepts. Places of entertainment are also closed so as not to distract the faithful from the task of contemplation!

Each Poya is different as it marks a different episode in the life of Buddha, or a specific event in the history of the religion, all of which are important milestones to practising Buddhists. Poya Days all have names, and some are considerably more important than others, due to the event in the Buddhist calendar which they commemorate.

In January, Duruthu Poya celebrates Buddha's first visit to Sri Lanka, while February's Navam Poya celebrates four events in Buddhist history: the naming of the two principal disciples—Ven Sariputta and Mogallana, the first Buddhist council, the setting up of Vinaya for the guidance of monks and the declaration of the 80-year-old Buddha that his life would end in three months. A temple in Colombo organises a *perahera* called Navam Perahera, which is a close second to the Kandy Perahera.

In March, Medin Poya commemorates the journey of the Buddha from Bihar back to his home in Kapilavastu in Nepal, to preach to his own family. April's Bak Poya celebrates the Buddha's second visit to Sri Lanka, five years after his enlightenment.

Vesak in May is the most sacred of the Poya Days, because it commemorates the three most significant events in the Buddhist calendar: the day Prince Siddhartha Gotama was born, the day that he attained Enlightenment and became the Buddha, and the day that he died, or attained *nirvana*. It is celebrated in a very special way which is discussed in more detail in the following section.

June's Poson Poya commemorates the introduction of Buddhism to Sri Lanka in the 2nd century BC; July's Esala Poya celebrates the arrival of the Buddha tooth relic in Sri Lanka and is the occasion for an enormous *perahera* (see explanation below) in Kandy. It is also the month when the three-month retreat for monks begins. Called *vas*, this tradition has come down directly from the time of Buddha, and provides a time for the renewing of vows and increased meditation. The *vas* period also coincides with the major monsoon that brings torrential rain to India and Sri Lanka. Nikini Poya in August is the Poya when those monks who did not take a vow to observe *vas* in July, do so.

In September, Binara Poya remembers Buddha's trip to a heavenly abode to preach to his mother and other immortal souls; October's Wap Poya marks the return of Buddha to earth and, as Prince Siddhartha, his renunciation of all material things. It also marks the end of the *vas* season for Buddhist monks.

November's Il Poya celebrates several things, such as the sending out of disciples by Buddha to spread his teachings, and finally in December, Unduvap Poya commemorates the arrival in Sri Lanka of the sapling of the sacred bo tree.

Many Poya days are marked by *peraheras* held in various parts of the country. *Perahera* is a Sinhalese word which technically means procession: a procession of any kind in fact. In practice, it refers more specifically to the long torch-lit processions commemorating Buddhist holy days.

Peraheras are usually organised by a specific temple and are participated in by the members of that temple community. They centre around the ceremonial exposition of some specific holy relic kept by the organising temple, accompanied by as sumptuous a display of finery and colour as the temple can muster.

A caparisoned elephant bearing a relic casket, preceded by a temple official in traditional attire.

Traditionally *peraheras* are held at night on the eve of the Poya day, but more lately, a trend has developed to repeat the *perahera* procession at least once during the day time—often, however, without using the same finery and certainly without the same impact that is created at night when the route of the procession is lighted solely by thousands of rush lamps placed along the way and carried by the participants.

The most famous of all *peraheras* takes place in Kandy on Esala Poya when hundreds of elephants, drummers, dancers and ordinary people in the most dazzling of costumes march through the streets, which takes several hours to pass. The centre of this particular *perahera* is the Temple of the Tooth. The tooth relic, believed to be a tooth of the Buddha and considered by Buddhists the world over to be the most sacred relic, is not taken in procession, though a *karanduwa* or casket closely resembling the one in which the relic is kept, is borne by the Maligawa elephant, majestically caprisioned and lit by jets.

So spectacular is the Kandy *perahera* that it is repeated over several nights, each night featuring a larger and longer procession than the one the night before. The Kandy *perahera* has tacitly become the standard by which all other *peraheras* are judged.

Vesak

Vesak is a specifically Buddhist festival, the most important Poya day in the calendar.

A common sight at dawn on this day is the steady stream of white-clad *sil* takers who spend the day in temples or meditation halls. Many of them make a special point of observing all eight of the Buddhist precepts from this day to the following day, which means that they can only take a cup of milkless tea or a brew of coriander and ginger from 12:00 pm onwards until they give up *sil*. Obtaining the greatest possible spiritual purity is of extreme importance on this day and enhancing the powers

Festival of Lights

Unlike the Sinhala New Year, Vesak is a very public festival, often known as the 'Festival of Lights'. Its predominant feature is the elaborate display of lights and lanterns erected outside every house, and the erection of lighted *pandals* or screens by the community depicting events from the life of the Buddha.

of concentration by reducing bodily desires is part of the method by which this spiritual purity can be achieved.

It is considered meritorious to give small gifts of food and drink to all who pass by during the festival, and it is a common occurrence while driving through the rural areas of Sri Lanka at this time to be stopped by groups of people in specially constructed stalls by the side of the road and to be offered something to eat and drink. This is called a *dansal* (from the Sinhala words *dane*, to give, and *sala*, a room) and confers merit on the giver, an extension of the merit to be gained during the rest of the year by giving food and the necessities of life to the Buddhist clergy.

The Precepts of Buddha

The basic five precepts are observed daily by conscientious Buddhists. The eight precepts are observed on Poya days by those who take *sil* and by those who opt to devote the day to religious practice. The ten precepts are observed by those who have given up the lay life but have not become *bhikkus* (Buddhist monks). The precepts are repeated after a stanza which affirms the fact that one takes the Buddha (Teacher), Dhamma (the Teaching), and the Sangha (the lineage of *bhikkus*) as one's refuge.

The Five Precepts

I undertake to observe the precept to abstain from:

- destroying the life of beings
- taking things not given
- sexual misconduct
- false and malicious speech and gossip
- spirituous drinks, malt liquors and wines and mind-altering drugs—foundations for heedlessness

The Eight Precepts

In addition to the five precepts I undertake to observe the precept to abstain from:

- taking food at an unreasonable time (i.e., solid food between 12:00 pm and dawn of the next day)
- dancing, singing, music and unseemly shows; from the use of garlands, perfumes and unguents; and from things that tend to beautify and adorn
- using high and luxurious seats

The Ten Precepts

The seventh precept is divided into two to make the seventh and eighth precepts, while the eighth above becomes the ninth precept. The tenth precept reads thus:

- I undertake to observe the precept to abstain from acceptance of gold and silver and all cash dealings

Sinhala and Tamil New Year

Unlike the Christian New Year, the timing of the Sinhala and Tamil New Year (formerly the Sinhala and Hindu New Year) is astrologically predicted. It actually occurs when the sun enters into the constellation of Aries, but in practice usually falls in the middle of the month of April.

This is the only time in the year when all businesses close without exception, and a general air of festivity prevails.

New Year ceremonies are usually private in nature, and although the family will gather together, outsiders are often invited. It is of supreme importance that all be clean and prepared for the advent of the New Year. After the final meal of the year has been prepared and eaten, the family will thoroughly clean and wash the house and themselves, after which no work will be done until the advent of the New Year and the preparation of the first ritual meal, which invariably contains the traditional *kiribath* (milk rice), long associated with beginnings.

After the first meal, children will offer betel to their elders as a mark of respect and kneel before them to ask forgiveness for any offences committed in the previous year. Then presents are often exchanged among family members—wrapped in the auspicious betel leaf if they are gifts of money—and new clothes are worn to start the New Year.

A few days after the actual New Year day, a special ceremony is held in which the senior member of the family (usually the father or grandfather) puts a drop or two of specially prepared oil on the heads of his family members to bring them good luck in the coming year. These New Year practices are traditional rather than religious in nature, and the same rituals are followed by the majority of all Sinhalese and Tamils, not just by members of a specific religious group—somewhat unusual for a Sri Lankan holiday!

Id-Ul-Fitr and Id-ul-Alha

The Muslim community in Sri Lanka is often less conspicuous than its Buddhist or Hindu counterparts, for their religion is much more a private matter than a public spectacle. Muslim festivals do centre around the mosque, but only as a place in which to say special prayers, the celebrations that accompany the festivals being traditionally held in the home rather than in the community at large.

There are two major festivals celebrated by the Muslims in Sri Lanka, and both of them occur in conjunction with longer periods of time in the Muslim calendar.

Id-Ul-Fitr, the larger of the two, occurs at the end of the fasting month (Ramadan), during which no Muslim may eat between sunrise and sunset. On the last day of the fasting month, special prayers are said in the mosque by each individual Muslim, new clothes are worn and traditional greetings are exchanged between religious brethren.

After prayers have been completed, two measures of rice are traditionally given out by the head of each family that can afford it to those less fortunate than themselves. The gift of rice should be presented first to close neighbours or blood relatives in need, but failing this, it can also be given to anybody who is perceived to be needy in the eyes of the donor. In some rural mosques, the rice is collected by the mosque and dispensed centrally to the poor people of the area, but in the urban areas, the donations are often made directly by the donor to the recipient. In conjunction with this aspect of Id-Ul-Fitr, the wealthy Muslim may also pracrise *Zakat*—the fourth of the five principles of Islam—and donate 2.5 per cent of his personal income to the poor for their welfare.

Id-Ul-Alha, the other Muslim religious festival, occurs on the tenth of the Haj month, the traditional period of time during which those Muslims who are fit and affluent enough observe the fifth precept of Islam, making the pilgrimage or Haj to Mecca to worship at the central mosque of the Islamic faith.

If the Haj has been undertaken in that year, special prayers are said in Mecca on this day, but if the individual is still in his own community, the prayers are said in the local mosque. After the prayers, some Muslims still observe the custom of *Korban*, or the ritual sacrifice to God. It may be a cow or a sheep or even some other animal that is sacrificed (though, of course, not a pig) and the cost of doing so is borne by the head of the household, who then distributes the meat from the carcass so that one third of it is given to his immediate family, one third to close relatives, and one third to the poor and needy of the community.

Milad un-Nabi—Prophet Mohammed's birthday too is a public holiday.

Thai Pongal and Deepavali

There are two major Hindu festivals during the year, held in January and October respectively.

Thai Pongal occurs on 14 January, when the first grains of the new paddy harvest are ceremoniously cooked in milk in a specially decorated new pot. The rice is allowed to boil up and spill over (*pongol* means boiling over), the direction of the spill indicating either good luck or bad luck for the family in the coming year.

Deepavali commemorates the day when evil was vanquished by Lord Vishnu and good was established in its place. As evil and goodness are represented in Hindu mythology by darkness and light, the festival is celebrated by the lighting of many lights in homes and in places of worship. A side effect of this practice is that the sky becomes brightly lit up at the time of the year when the sun is traditionally weakest. It is usually held at the end of October or the beginning of November. Hindus celebrate their New Year in April on the same two days as the Sinhala New Year.

Christmas

Christmas is celebrated by the large number of Sri Lankan Christians. Religious observances are very similar to those in the West, but the commercial aspect is less in evidence.

The non-religious aspects are celebrated with gusto by all: Christmas trees of many varieties and homes brightly decorated and the traditional paraphernalia of the Christmas season. This is also the time of the year for present giving, which for expatriates usually means not only to their families, but also to servants, tradesmen and service people who come to the house during the year.

BEGINNINGS AND ENDS

Sri Lankans love celebrating, so something new is always an occasion for communal rejoicing: be it a new baby, a new venture, a new job or simply the start of something new and, hopefully, exciting.

To ensure a lucky and propitious start of any kind, a special celebration is held to make sure that the beginning is as auspicious as possible. *Kiribath* (milk rice) and *jaggery* (the sap of the kitul palm which tastes surprisingly like caramel fudge) are prepared, and a special decoration is made of the coconut flower for the table on which the food and drink to be served is laid, and around which the ceremony is to take place.

The ceremony itself is quite simple: an initial verbal welcome to the guests from the host, followed by a short speech from one of the invited dignitaries wishing the new person or enterprise well. A traditional brass lamp of a special Sri Lankan design is then lit by the chief guest and he and the important guests are then presented with betel leaves, signifying respect for their presence.

Glasses of water are passed around to indicate that the meal will be served, and that all are invited to share in the food prepared for the occasion. It is polite to touch the glass to show that the invitation has been accepted and that the guest joins in the general well-wishing.

Each guest is expected to take at least one piece of milk rice and *jaggery* and join in the general conversation that ensues over the eating and drinking. After this, the special invitees usually take their leave and the party begins in earnest! Needless to say, the days on which such occasions are held are often special holidays for those directly concerned with the event which is being celebrated!

The end of the venture is not celebrated in such a high key (as might be expected) but, if it is something that has been going on for a long time, a gathering will be held to commemorate the project and to say goodbye to those who have participated in it. There are no formal ceremonies and the nature of the party that ensues will naturally depend on the mood of the participants. Funerals do have special rites (*see* Chapter Four: Socialising with the Locals *on page 71*).

VACATION TIME

For most expatriates, Colombo is the centre of their Sri Lankan world. Even if they don't live there most of the time—and the majority of expatriates do anyway—Colombo will usually be the focus of their social and cultural life. But there is a lot more to Sri Lanka than Colombo, and everyone

Peaceful, cool, crisp country in the mountains—an ideal vacation spot.

itches from time to time to indulge in the sybaritic pleasures of cooling off in the hills or suntanning on the beach. Neither of these is difficult to do and both of them are relatively inexpensive. Resident expatriates could negotiate discounts in tourist hotels and when visiting museums etc since they are not foreign tourists per se. In addition to hotels, there are numerous houses and bungalows owned by individuals and the government which can be rented, along with servants, for modest sums indeed.

Apart from the individually-owned bungalows (listed in an excellent, though hard to find, publication called *Accommodation in Sri Lanka*) which can be rented by direct negotiation with the owner, a number of government offices (especially the Forestry and Wildlife Departments) have attractively situated houses which they rent to those who book them in advance through their Colombo offices. It is important to remember, however, that the main use of these accommodations is as 'circuit bungalows', or places for visiting officers to stay when travelling out of Colombo on business. As a result, these bungalows are not always available for the public at large, and can only be booked when they are not being used by the department concerned for their own purposes.

Yala National Park, Horton Plains Natural Reserve and Singharaja Rain Forest Preserve all have such accommodation—of varying degrees of comfort—and it is often available at short notice, always provided that arrangements to rent it have been made in advance. The Ceylon Hotels Corporation also runs a very good network of rest houses throughout the country, which combined with a network of privately owned rest houses (some still fairly primitive) means that there is usually somewhere acceptable to stay no matter where you may wish to travel on the island.

Of course, from time to time, the inevitable claustrophobia of living on an island—no matter how beautiful—strikes the temporary resident, and it becomes time to escape for a while to another location. Bangkok, Singapore and South India are all close and inexpensive to reach by air.

LANGUAGES AND BODY TALK

CHAPTER 8

'Their language is Copious, Smooth, Elegant, Courtly:
accordingly the people that speak it are. In their speech
the people are bold without sheepish shame facedness,
and yet no more confidence than is becoming.
The worst word they use to Whites and Christians
is to call them beef-eating slaves!'
—Robert Knox

COMMUNICATING WITH SRI LANKANS

Understanding Sri Lanka and Sri Lankans comes as much from an understanding of how Sri Lankan communication works as it does from understanding the spoken languages themselves. There are several verbal languages and dialects which Sri Lankans use to communicate to each other and to outsiders: Sinhala, Tamil and English are the most common, but there are also a number of unspoken ways in which messages, just as important as those that are spoken, are conveyed from one person to another.

The way that Sri Lankans move, the gestures that they use, the traditional actions which come as second nature to those who have grown up in the island can all be baffling to someone unaccustomed to them, and an understanding of their meaning and their importance in the Sri Lankan community is essential to a happy and productive stay in the country.

SPOKEN LANGUAGES

Sinhala is the main language. There is no unanimous agreement as to the origins of the Sinhala language, as some scholars suggest that it does not have an affinity with any other language, having developed spontaneously in the island itself. However, it seems most likely that Sinhala is a derivation from the original Indo-European group of languages from which, through different branches, came some modern

European languages, including English and the ancient Asian languages of Sanskrit and Pali (the languages of Hinduism and Buddhism). Modern Sinhala is most closely linked to these two languages, linguistically and semantically. The multi-volumed *Sinhala Dictionary*, including the etymology of Sinhala words, traces most words to Pali and Sanskrit roots.

Like a number of other Asian languages, the script of written Sinhala is very like that used in Pali writings and has no direct phonological relation to the spoken language. In fact, it is possible to learn spoken Sinhala to quite an advanced level, but not be able to read a word of it! To the uninitiated, Sinhala writing looks like a totally unintelligible scribble of loops and strokes, but it is in fact a very highly developed and flexible method of recording ideas.

Whatever language Sinhala may have derived from, and despite its similarities in derivation to some other area languages, including Maldivian, Sinhala has some very distinctive characteristics of its own.

For instance, the Sinhala view of the world is not a two-fold one—'over there or over here'—but a four-folded one. According to the best book available on learning to speak Sinhala, J B Disanayake's *Say It in Sinhala*, things in Sinhala can be 'that over there', 'that away from us', 'this near me' or 'this near you'! Logical minded English speakers might have some difficulty in figuring out exactly what these esoteric shades of meaning actually denote! Sinhala also sometimes uses only one word where English uses more than one. One 'drinks' a liquid and 'smokes' a cigarette; in Sinhala, the word to describe these two actions is exactly the same: *bonawa*!

Tamil has a quite different origin from Sinhala, and there are few links between the two. The origins of the Tamil language lie in South India, where Tamil is spoken widely, and where the original inhabitants were of Dravidian rather than Aryan stock.

The Tamil language first came to Sri Lanka over 20 centuries ago with the migration south of Tamils over the Palk Strait, from the area now known as Tamil Nadu, to settle in the northern part of the island. In fact, the Tamil language now spoken in Sri Lanka has really become a dialect of Indian Tamil as changes have taken place in the language here that have not happened elsewhere, and vice versa.

Road signs are extra large to accommodate three languages.

Like Sinhala, written Tamil differs from spoken Tamil—and is just as unintelligible to the uninitiated, even if they have learned to speak the language! Such similarities as there are between Sinhala and Tamil are not linguistic but cultural, and lie mainly in words that have been imported into the two languages from a third language, rather than in any fundamental linguistic similarity.

It is not the intention of this book to become a primer on either Sinhala or Tamil, but a little knowledge of how each language works goes a long way, both towards picking up a few words of a local language for survival on the street and understanding how the Sri Lankan mind actually works, if that were possible! The glossary at the back of the book on page 190 should start you out in the right direction.

UNSPOKEN LANGUAGE

It was said earlier that what is expressed without language in Sri Lanka is as important as that for which there are words. Nowhere is this more true than in the way that Sri Lankans use body language.

Anyone who has been to Sri Lanka for even a few days has met the traditional Sri Lankan head waggle or woggle. At first glance, it seems something like the headshake that Western speakers use to express the negative, but on closer examination, the motion, though similar, is not quite the same. In a Western headshake, the whole head is moved from side to side, while a Sri Lankan moves his head a shorter distance each way to the side and at the same time slightly up and down. It's quite a difficult motion to accomplish—try it!—but second nature to every Sri Lankan who uses it to express agreement, often accompanied by the sound 'Hah'. This gesture is extremely common and very disconcerting at first, though after a while easy to get used to.

In addition to the head waggle, Sri Lankan gestures include a 'come hither' motion made with the hand, moving it downwards with fingers pointing inwards, while the arm is extended in front of the body—a gesture that many Westerners consider to be the classic 'get lost' signal!

Incidentally, holding hands is quite common between members of the same sex, though somewhat frowned upon by the older generation whose native understanding has been somewhat tempered by the superimposition of colonial British standards. Heterosexual handholding is not common in public, though it is taking on now with young adults feeling freer and getting to know they have rights! A stroll down Galle Face Green on a weekend or a glance into the back row of any local cinema might give a totally different impression.

THE SIGNIFICANCE OF NAMES

Many Sri Lankans have a *ge* (pronounced 'gay') name which is an important part of their identity. The *ge* name is bestowed at birth and is peculiar to the paternal side of the family. It prefixes the given name and the surname. For example, the co-author's *ge* name is Dunukara Mudiyanselage—which translates to 'of the Leader of the archers'.

In ancient Sri Lanka, these names were often related to the caste or traditional occupation of the male family members, and may later serve as surnames. After the occupation of Sri Lanka by three successive colonising powers (Portugal, Holland and Britain) and the imposition by them of their own surnames on the local population (which accounts for the phenomenal numbers of Pereras, Fernandos and De Silvas in Sri Lanka), the use of *ge* names began to diminish, with

Ge names are often very long and cumbersome to use, but they are a distinguishing mark of individuality, and tend to survive among those Sri Lankans who are most traditional or most proud of their heritage.

the result that some Sri Lankans no longer have them, and those that do use them rarely.

Other Sri Lankan naming peculiarities come from a more rigid definition of the extended family structure than the Westerner might be used to. For example, there are specific words in Sinhala used to describe each of the relationships in a family, ranging from 'older sister' and 'younger sister' all the way to 'father's great aunt' and even to 'cousin-brother', a way of defining a loose family relationship with another male of the same generation.

These terms are also often used in a general sense to identify informal relationships with someone whose name is not known, e.g. the child of a stranger, or a bus conductor addressing a passenger (an annoying habit!). Their meaning often breaks down when translated into a language that does not have the same flexibility to describe complex relationships. For example, most unrelated children are addressed by their possible relationship (e.g. an older girl might be called *Akka*, 'older sister' by a younger one) or by the general 'baby', an epithet that used to throw my 13-year-old daughter—to whom it was applied in a friendly tone by strangers on the street—into fits of righteous indignation until she learnt how loose the actual meaning of it was!

SPACING YOURSELF

The Buddhist tradition of respect in Sri Lanka often determines the degree of elevation of a superior person over an inferior. The greater the elevation, the greater the respect in which the person is held: an idea which results from the tradition of raising the Buddhist monk above those with whom he is communicating and from the traditional method of showing respect for an elder or superior by bowing low at his feet.

Some people contend that this idea has been added through the British educational tradition, prevalent in colonial Ceylon and still observed in many places today, of placing the teacher at the front of the class, and in many cases on a raised dais—though this, of course, has nothing to do with

Buddhism! Whatever the truth of the origins, respect today is still conveyed by space, either the amount of it accorded to somebody or the elevation at which he must be regarded.

Ironically enough, just the reverse is true in determining the degree of distance between two friends.

Personal distances between two friends of the same sex in Sri Lanka tend to be less than in the West. Like a lot of other Eastern cultures, conversations are often held while standing very close to the other person, and most Sri Lankans will tolerate a much more densely packed environment (such as in a crowded bus) for far longer than most Westerners will. Touching is also more common among friends than in the West, and a regular occurrence where babies and children are concerned.

The only exceptions to this rule occur in contact between the sexes where contact is much more circumspect. It is not polite to shake a lady's hand, for instance, until she extends it to you, and as far as touching (including kissing) in any other way is concerned, this is very strictly reserved as a more intimate form of affection—and then only in private! Kissing in greeting and departing—the peck on the cheek—is more a low country habit. Kandyans usually greet each other and say their goodbyes with space in between, by placing palms together in Indian *namaste* fashion. One bends from the waist when the greeting is to an elder or better. Monks and respected older relations have the layperson or young one kneeling and placing hands together.

KEEPING IN TIME
Sri Lankan time is considerably more relaxed and flexible than Western time. In fact, time itself is almost a relative concept—relative to the amount of daylight, manpower, urgency and desire to get something accomplished. This can also mean that temporal concepts, such as 'tomorrow' or 'in half an hour' are also relative, and not necessarily to be understood as strict indicators of the actual amount of time that is needed.

The impact on the foreigner of this approach to time-keeping can be a frustrating one, especially if the sense

of urgency felt by the Westerner has not been understood or regarded by the other party. For instance, many things promised to be done at a certain time are not finished at that time, thus necessitating a second and even sometimes a third visit. To avoid this kind of frustration, it is necessary to do as most Sri Lankans do. Accept the inevitable and resign yourself to the fact that things will get done given time—even if the time taken is longer than you would like it to be.

The imprecision of time is also evident in the hours at which things start and finish. An invitation for an informal dinner at 7:30 pm does not mean, as it does in some Western countries, that you should be there no later than 7:30 pm, but rather that you should not arrive before, and preferably later. In some—admittedly rare—cases, informal functions that were supposed to start at 7:30 pm have not got off the ground until 10:00 pm! If the function happens to include a meal, it is sometimes wise to have a snack before going.

Formal functions and other events more precise in their nature, such as the start of a concert, happen more or less on

Colourful sights and sounds will greet you at markets in Sri Lanka. It is common to see fresh vegetables and fruits placed on the floor by vendors.

Two monks stand before a massive statue of Buddha, which dates back to the 12th century, in the ancient city of Polonnaruwa.

A rock pool lies above the spectacular Diyaluma Falls, which is the second highest waterfall in Sri Lanka.

Children enjoy a game of cricket on a street in Kandy while the adults watch. Cricket is undoubtedly a highly popular sport among Sri Lankans from young to old.

Female tea-pickers collect tea leaves at a plantation in Nuwara Eliya. The tea industry is one of Sri Lanka's top earners.

time, but there is almost always a 5 or 10-minute delay even here—as if precision were something that actually militates against the much more *laissez-faire* attitude to time-keeping that characterises Sri Lanka.

THE IMPORTANCE OF FACE

The importance of keeping face with others is a very widespread concept, particularly so in Asia, and thus it is no stranger to Sri Lanka. 'Face' is somewhat akin to the Western idea of personal dignity, or reputation among others, and being made to lose face in a public situation is a very serious matter for any individual.

Unfortunately, face is easy to lose and any number of perfectly ordinary situations can lead to a loss of face, if not handled sensitively. For example, criticism of a junior employee by a senior one, if that dressing down takes place in front of his peers, would cause a loss of face, as might the refusal to accept the help of someone offering it spontaneously or even paid to give it—ignoring offered assistance in finding the way when travelling, or rejecting the services of the bellboy in a hotel for example.

Losing face, in fact, is inherent in every situation in which someone suffers a loss of personal dignity, a situation which can be created consciously through ignorance of the importance of face or unconsciously by some form of unwitting rejection of someone who is only trying to help. In any event, no one likes to lose face, and many people will go to inordinate lengths to avoid such a situation.

> The surest way to lose an argument with anybody in Sri Lanka is to force him into a position from which he cannot retreat without a loss of dignity. This requires the complete abandonment of confrontational tactics, which never work in a situation in which there is a risk to the person being confronted with loss of face.

Ironically enough, perhaps to counter the inaction that can be brought on by fear of losing face, a streak of pragmatism also runs through most Sri Lankans. The first reaction might be to attribute mishaps to others or to worry about losing face if they attempt to solve the problem and fail. However, if the problem is of a practical nature (such as having to provide a special repair job), the ingenuity of most Sri Lankans soon asserts itself and the initial 'What to do?' is often followed by a strong outburst of 'Oh, well let's get on and get it fixed'—as long as a solution, no matter how temporary, can be identified! Sri Lankans are nothing if not practical, and although things may go wrong with greater frequency than they would in the developed world, there are also some very ingenious solutions possible in situations that might seem insoluble to the more pragmatic expatriate!

In Sri Lanka, the fear of losing a battle and thus losing face manifests itself in many ways, the most common being the tendency to avoid making any kind of decision which has a chance of being wrong. Very often, it is difficult to find out who the decision-makers are in Sri Lankan offices or businesses, because, for obvious reasons, they prefer not to be immediately identifiable. If they were obvious, there would be a tendency for confrontation to take place in situations where tempers are aroused. So most decisions are arrived at indirectly. Requests for a decision are made to an underling and then passed along the chain of command until the decision is made somewhere not obviously traceable; only then is it relayed back to the requester by the same underling to whom it was made.

Of course, the drawback to this system is that getting anything done takes a long time—a visit to a Sri Lankan government office can often be a very exhausting process, because of the sheer number of people who have to be consulted before a decision can be reached. However, there is an improvement in certain offices. The Immigration and Emigration office in Punchi Borella (Colombo 8) functions efficiently notwithstanding the crowds that have to be served, mostly on passport business. The telecommunication department is another department that, privatised and calling itself Sri Lanka Telecom (SLT), gives very good service.

WHAT TO DO?

The expression 'What to do?' is often the Sri Lankan's response to an unusual situation. It does not necessarily indicate that nothing can be done if there is a problem. Quite the reverse, for what this expression most usually indicates is that a pause is called for to think of possible solutions to the problem; a thinking process sometimes—and rather disconcerting to the foreigner—said out loud, either to himself or to anyone who happens to be standing near by.

The question 'What to do?' when said aloud, does not, in most cases, require an answer; it is rhetorical. Often, it is used as consolation, when one loses something or even someone in death. Here it is really not a question but a mere acceptance of fate. The 'what to do' in such an event of loss is often accompanied by the sentiment: 'That is life.'

DOING BUSINESS IN SRI LANKA

'Nor is it held any disgrace for Men of the greatest quality to do any work either at home or in the field, if it be for themselves: to work for hire with them is reckoned for great shame: and very few here are found that will work so.'
—Robert Knox

BUSINESS, THE SRI LANKAN WAY

There is often a tacit assumption that the skills of doing business successfully are basically the same the world over with small regional variations that, while not tremendously important, are easily mastered. This is a very persistent myth in fact, the falsity of which often only becomes apparent after a series of spectacular failures. American businessmen who applied Western strategies and frames of reference to doing business in Arab countries or the emerged Chinese market have found to their cost that the way that business is conducted in those countries is very different from the way that most business deals are wrought in the United States.

Sri Lanka has its own variants—perhaps less obvious on the surface because of the country's apparent Westernisation—and the businessman or entrepreneur who approaches the Sri Lankan businessmen totally unprepared for them will often find himself baffled by a lack of understanding of exactly what these variants are.

EXPECTATIONS

By and large, purely Sri Lankan firms do not employ expatriate staff, since the expertise necessary for running their business is available in the country. Expatriates are found generally in three situations. One is where the firm is a Sri Lankan branch of a foreign firm and the parent firm might, if they so desire, have expatriates working in the Sri Lanka operation. The second is where there is a development project undertaken with part or whole foreign financing; here the foreign funding entity generally has expatriates employed in certain positions on the project. The third is the area of technical assistance. Some international schools and the British Council English teaching section employ expatriate, mostly British, teachers. In all three situations, what Sri Lankan workers expect most is that the foreigner be able to do the job at least as well as, if not better than, a Sri Lankan would be able to do it. INGOs are another case in point that employ a couple of expatriates, or just one, with all other officers being local.

The foreigner is also bound to run into a certain amount of resentment where there is a perception among the Sri Lankans either that one of them could do the job equally well, if not better, and/or that the foreigner has taken away a job that belongs to one of them. Given the current level of unemployment, this is perhaps not a totally unfounded resentment, especially given a foreigner's usually superior working and living conditions. In fact, many organisations have only one expatriate member of staff and so one's working colleagues will all be Sri Lankan nationals. This is both a blessing and a drawback, for it is difficult to know initially exactly what kind of a relationship will develop between the expatriate and the Sri Lankan, and the onus will be very much on the expatriate for the first few months to prove that he or she intends to be a member of a team, and not someone who has been parachuted in from outside.

Similarly, there are businesses and commercial enterprises in Sri Lanka which are family based. These will naturally have members of the family in sensitive and key positions, and they are very conscious of preserving the Sri Lankan family unit in the appointments that they make. While an expatriate is probably unlikely to be directly employed by one of these firms, if contact with one becomes a business necessity, it is as well to remember that the central core of the business revolves around the unity of family members rather than loyalty to outside individuals. Even in some multinationals, the element of 'family first' is still evident!

From the moment he enters Sri Lanka, the foreigner will, on various occasions during the course of work and stay, have to deal with Sri Lankan officials. He would do well initially to invest a little time in finding out who is in charge of the subject of his concern as an executive in the Government Ministries and Departments. He should then be prepared to deal with that official, and get used to his or her working practice. He should also realise that in any government or private entrepreneurial bureaucracy, officials at different levels have different decision-making powers—or, to put it another way, have decision-making powers that cover only certain areas. Therefore, the official he deals with may or may not be able to give him a decision right away, and referral to a higher authority or official may prove necessary.

This bureaucratic familiarisation process could conceivably be done by a company Sri Lankan liaison officer or someone holding a similar position in the organisation. However, it is important to realise that Sri Lankan departments will deal with enterprises on any subject at the same level of operation as the officer they send to deal with it. Thus a clerk sent to a government office will only be able to get information from another clerk, and, if information is required from a senior level, a senior person from the firm wanting the information must be sent to get it.

The Sri Lankan Entrepreneur

There appears to be no limit to the ingenuity of the Sri Lankan entrepreneur. Quite aside from the large, well-established companies whose names are synonymous with the growth of Sri Lanka as a business centre (John Keells, Cargills, Elephant House), there are a myriad of small businesses to be found everywhere, involved in every conceivable type of activity.

Colombo's traditional trading centre, the Pettah, is still today as much a hive of activity of small traders and entrepreneurs going about their daily business as it has been in years gone by. The rice traders sit in Old Moor Street with their sample bowls of different grades, while the 'tinkers' sell shiny everyday utensils from open-fronted shops hung with samples of their wares.

Even outside Colombo, the entrepreneurial spirit can be found in locations as diverse as large trading houses, small shops, in the hulk of an old lorry used as a tyre repair centre or even on a bicycle selling brooms. Making one's own living is so much a way of life for many Sri Lankans that they would not part with it lightly, and even the most modest of profits allow the entrepreneurial spirit to thrive unabated through troubled economic times.

A small shop selling everything from rice and pulses, to bottled jams, cordials and canned drinks—a typical Sri Lankan small business.

WORK AND REAL LIFE

In Sri Lanka, the predominant style of work is a combination of the British colonial legacy and a natural rhythm of life that is typically Sri Lankan. In colonial times, it was the expatriate who led and the local who followed, with the inevitable result that most of the decisions were made at a level above that of the Sri Lankans, and as part of a process in which they were not encouraged to participate. This generalisation, of course, admitted of quite a few exceptions, especially as the average colonial Sri Lankan tended to be much more highly educated than his Indian counterpart to the north—but the rule of thumb did lead to a mentality in many where work and 'real life' became totally separate.

Work became a necessity for earning an income to support the family, while real life comprised the time which was not spent in the office or factory, and the activities within that time. This division is reinforced in many contemporary Sri Lankan attitudes to work. Among middle management and below, this can be seen to some extent in the amount of time that is actually expended on work as compared with the amount of time that is spent on social life.

There is, in fact, generally a much greater relaxation over work time schedules in Sri Lanka than in the West. As mentioned in an earlier chapter, Westerners often speak laughingly of 'Sri Lanka time', which always seems to run more slowly than 'Western' time. However, this does not mean that there is no sense of time among the people, but just that the sense of time is different. In a society that has evolved fairly quickly from agrarian to commercial, the attitude to time is naturally more elastic.

There are several implications of this elasticity of time: getting to work, for instance. Roads and public transport are congested in the mornings and in the evenings with people getting in and out of the city. Infrastructural development has not kept pace with the growth of the demands made on it. The result is that traffic does not flow smoothly at peak hours, and people travelling at this time might expect to arrive late (not necessarily habitually, but it does happen), particularly if they travel some distance to the city, which more and more people are doing these days.

Then again, some of the services that are taken for granted in the West, like each school having its own bus service for the smaller children, are not found in Sri Lanka. There is a school bus service, run by the Transport Board, which caters for the schools—individually or collectively—but it does not belong to the schools, nor does it pick up individual schoolchildren belonging to a particular school. As a result, very small children do not travel on these buses unless accompanied by an older brother or sister, or in the particular charge of someone. Generally, in these situations, a parent (usually the one who goes to work) takes the child to school on his or her way to work. The other parent or a neighbour brings the child home from school. Schools start an hour or so before offices open, but it is indicative of the pressure on traffic at this time of the day that someone whose responsibilities involve delivering a child to school might arrive late at his job without any sense of guilt.

An observer will also notice that, though the working day ends at 4:30 or 5:00 pm, some offices close even earlier. This is to enable people to get home in the less crowded times, but even then public transportation out of the city is crowded until 7:00 pm or later. Also, some workers do their grocery shopping after work, some attend meetings or meet friends, or spend time in recreational clubs, yet others have their happy hour (or hour and half!).

There is also the widespread practice of the availability of 'short leave', a time generally taken twice a month, when an employee can legitimately leave one or two hours early

to attend to personal business with no penalty expected or given. There is a logical reason for this, in fact, and it is not unconnected with the division between work and 'real life'. Many things in Sri Lanka take longer to accomplish than they do elsewhere, and there are occasions when these practicalities may cause a delay in a regular routine.

The foreigner will see that in Sri Lanka, there is no inordinate hurry on the part of people merely to get something done. If a rush job of work has to be done, the job will be done as expected, but normally, the foreigner will have to get used to a more relaxed and less rushed framework of operations than he would have been used to in his own country.

An office messenger was always on time except for the last day of every month, when he was consistently late. On being challenged about this, his explanation was simple: the last day of the month was when the season tickets for the bus on which he travelled to work were issued, and the queue was such a long one that it could take up to two hours to buy a ticket. In Sri Lanka, such a situation is not unusual and no matter for comment.

This does not mean that the foreigner has suddenly found himself in the land of lotus or opium eaters, or even layabouts, though indeed, examples of all three are to be found in the land. Nor need the foreigner have apprehensions about the efficiency of his Sri Lankan workers and counterparts, or fear that his profits will take a nose dive. None of the foreign enterprises in the country has been heard to complain on either score. Moreover, if the foreigner were to look around him, he would see instances of some very innovative technology at the ordinary technician level: cars that are a decade or two or more old, but are still kept going in quite a satisfactory fashion, electrical repair shops which will replace a burnt out winding on your fan, doing it by hand... and so on. This does not exactly point to either lotus or opium eating, but simply that the foreigner has to get used to a different tempo of life and work.

An aside may be slipped in here. It has been found by many employers that women are much more conscientious, duty bound workers at all levels. There is however a 'but' in this situation: the spirit of entrepreneurship is, in general, submerged or even lacking in women, unlike in the male.

Transacting personal and social business in company time is a much more acceptable practice in Sri Lanka than it would be in the West. The main reason for its widespread tolerance is the problem of personal communication, and there are several manifestations of its existence that are apparent in the workplace.

In a country where telephone costs are very high and not everyone has the facility—though cell phones are ubiquitous even in this Third World country—many people take the opportunity to make arrangements and appointments when they are at work. Another contributory factor, specially in the case of a woman employee, is that she simply has no time to make telephone calls while at home. As long as this practice does not become excessive or start to interfere with an employee's productivity to too great a degree, it is usually tacitly tolerated. In some places, personal calls are required to be recorded, and the cost recovered later, but these calls are usually the ones that it is necessary to make, and not the calls to talk about last night's party or so-and-so's wedding.

Again, because of the lack of access to a telephone or, more probably, sheer indifference in the case of employees at a lower rung, there are sometimes occasions when an employee will not report for work for a whole day without forewarning, and quite unabashedly deal with something that is of consummate personal importance in his 'real life'—the logic of which in the employee's mind will be quite clearly apparent to the boss.

For much the same reason, personal business appointments are rarely made in some circles, the expectations being that one can 'drop in' to see the person whom one wants to contact and see him when he is free, just as one would in 'real life'. As a local businessman put it, 'waiting is a way of life in Sri Lanka', to the extent that if someone is busy or absent, it is not uncommon to find people quite prepared to settle down to a two or three-hour wait until such time as it is convenient for that person to see them, or a substitute officer is available.

Within the office itself, business and social life mix in what might be the Sri Lankan equivalent of congregation round the office water cooler or coffee machine. As Sri Lankan offices do not usually have water coolers, a cup of tea is usually brought round in the mid-morning and the mid-afternoon, and this is a sacred time. When on a tea break, the worker is strictly 'off duty' and does not expect to have to deal with work-related matters—even if he is seated at his desk. This is the time for non-business interaction (as is to be expected in any group of people who spend eight hours a day and five days a week in each other's company) and the worker treats it as such, the time ending when the 'break' is deemed to be over and 'real life' is replaced by the necessities of work.

Social activities aside, there are also the relatively rare occasions when religious rites intersect with the day to day running of a place of business. As will be remembered from the section on festivals, there are special occasions when religious ceremonies could be appropriately held in the workplace. The special ceremony to mark beginnings is an obvious example of this and the chanting of special prayers on such an auspicious occasion might give rise to one instance when work would cease temporarily. A more regular occurrence would concern Muslim employees only, whose weekly special prayer time falls between noon and 2:00 pm on Fridays, and when they might well be absent from their place of employment to join in the prayers at the mosque.

ABSENTEEISM

The foreigner will soon realise that certain things he would take for granted back home do not exist in Sri Lanka, like day-care centres attached to work places. He will also need to take into account certain prevalent social practices in various fields.

For instance, an employee of his may not report for work and would be tardy in giving timely notice of his absence. If for example the employee finds his wife or child sick when he wakes up in the morning, he may take the ill person to the doctor, and then call up his office or send a message through a colleague. With almost everyone possessing cell phones (even the garbage collector and the house maid), lack of communication of this sort is infrequent now. But it does happen, more due to the habit of giving family first place and those holding lower-responsibility jobs still harbouring laissez faire attitudes to their employment. The result of this would sometimes be referred to as absenteeism.

The foreigner would ask here why the sick wife could not go to the doctor's by herself, or could not take the sick child. This could be done, and sometimes is done. But the other scenario where the husband needs to get involved also exists. There is no hard and fast rule. The foreigner will have to attune himself to the practice of different employees and colleagues. There is no point asking why Mr Y's wife cannot go to the doctor's by herself, when Mr X's wife does so. In the social situation that exists in the country, both patterns of conduct are accepted as equally valid. Indeed, among the more traditional elements of society, the first pattern would be the more regular one. And the traditional elements of society could be found at any level.

There are also other occasions when people may need to be absent from their workplaces for short periods of time during the working day. The payment of bills, particularly bills for services (water, electricity, etc.) is another chore that many Sri Lankans are

The foreigner would do well to assess each situation in the light of practices that prevail in Sri Lanka and not on the basis of what might be done in his own country in a similar situation. Of course, he should be on the lookout at the same time for the time-waster and truant.

in the habit of doing personally. There are, indeed, those who make payment by cheque sent by mail, as in other countries, or through banks that offer such services. Once again, both ways of doing it coexist. Indeed, the service organisations have facilitated matters for those who wish to attend personally to the payment of their bills by designating specific branches of banks where this may be done.

BECOMING AN EFFECTIVE SRI LANKAN BOSS

The management style appropriate to adopt in Sri Lanka will, of course, depend to a large extent on the individual, his function, and the size of the organisation for which he is working. In Sri Lanka, the boss is very much the boss and as such is expected to make the decisions.

Input for decisions taken can be solicited and will be given—with some hesitation in case it leads to a situation in which face is at stake—but the actual decision will be quite clearly delineated as that of the boss and the consequences of that decision, whatever they may be, will be his as well. Thus there is a certain reluctance to take decisions at lower levels of management, particularly in the public service, and some decisions that could have been made at a lower level may well be referred to the boss for decision to prevent others from losing face. Similarly, the boss's own face has to be protected by his subordinates and thus he is unlikely to be told if his decision has a serious flaw in it because of something that he might not have been aware of.

Consideration, compassion and understanding of the complex cultural patterns of the country are obviously all important in establishing and maintaining harmonious personal and trusting relationships.

The concept of honesty, too, is one that suffers from differences in cultural perspective. The Sri Lankan worker is by and large not dishonest, but payoffs and kickbacks are a fairly common practice and one in which no harm is seen. The fact that they are received will, therefore, not necessarily be hidden from the boss, but the boss is going to have to decide what to do about their existence and to what extent they might create a conflict of interest. It should also be realised that there may well be some hidden kickbacks too; these will have to be dealt with as they occur.

The criteria for judgement of one's fellow employees at the workplace has to be based on the same kind of management rules that apply in the West, but with a tolerance and understanding for the hidden agendas that sometimes produce unusual results. The only times at which such a basis for judgement might have to be suspended is when dealing with political appointees—of which there are many in the public service—or with relatives in a private company, a practice which is also fairly widespread.

If you come to Sri Lanka expecting less from your employees than you would normally from workers at home, you will not be disappointed, but you might be surprised at how much actually does get done when the socialising that goes on in the office is taken into account.

The Auspicious Time
Astrology plays a significant part in the lives of numerous people in Sri Lanka. Drawing up horoscopes is practised by a significant number of the population. This practice could also extend into the field of business transactions. Important appointments, meetings and negotiations could be arranged with the auspicious time, date or period in mind. Also, certain times, dates or periods would be avoided if they were considered inauspicious for work or negotiations in connection with an important venture. It is unlikely that these reasons will be cited when arrangements are being made, but you would do well to keep them in mind.

POLITICISATION
Over the years, the administration in Sri Lanka has seen more and more political appointments at various levels. It might

be well, therefore, for the foreigner to find out beforehand, as best he can, whether the particular official he is dealing with is a regular member of an administrative service or is a political appointee. There is a third possibility in between these two. Sri Lankans being highly politically conscious persons, there could be, in the cadre of any regular administrative service, permanent or career officials who have a strong leaning towards one political party or another, and are accepted by the parties concerned as officers they could fully rely on as being on their side. It could happen that, when a particular party gets voted into power, they will appoint such officials to key or sensitive positions in the administration.

Such practices would doubtless not be unfamiliar to foreigners from countries where they exist. But in Sri Lanka, which started off at independence with independent, career-oriented administrative services, these developments have aroused general controversy.

CORRUPTION

Charges of corruption are levelled from time to time by all sorts of people against both politicians and the administration. Editorials are written by newspapers on the subject. Indeed, among politicians at campaigning time, the matter is raised in one form or another. However, not all these charges are specific or backed up by valid evidence. However, corruption has increased and is a scourge, no denying that fact.

There is a Bribery Commissioner who investigates charges of bribery, and punitive measures are taken against anyone found guilty of corruption (both giving and receiving). While not attempting to paint the country and its people white (real or sepulchral), it has to be pointed out that in a developing country where levels of literacy and education and political consciousness are high, and levels of lawfully accumulated wealth—to a very great extent—modest, the unlawful accumulation of wealth draws a lot of attention. So, the foreigners versed in the ways of friendly persuasion that exist in the international corporate community would do well to take heed of all this.

WOMEN IN THE WORKPLACE

Sri Lanka has a very positive attitude to women in the workplace; after all, it was the first country in the world to have a female prime minister, and there are now several prominent women in government service.

At virtually every level of employment, from the lowliest upwards, women have found a place alongside men in the workforce, on occasions even outperforming their male counterparts. There are a few areas of employment, though, into which women have not yet ventured, such as engine drivers, guards, airline pilots, ship's captains or crew. Teapicking, however, is still almost an exclusively female job, as is machine minding in the multitude of garment factories. The glass ceiling has definitely been broken in the public sector, but not so in the private sector.

Sri Lanka does have its share of male chauvinists and those who think a woman's place is the home. Sexual harassment in the workplace is also at a much higher—and less sophisticated—level than would be tolerated in the West. But these attitudes are among the minority. Women are accepted in the workplace as equals and treated as such. There is no wage differentiation between men and women employees, the emoluments paid being equal. Certainly in government service, there can be no differentiation since the salary scale is fixed for the post, regardless of the sex of the holder.

Maternity leave arrangements are considered important; ILO standards are followed. The public sector does not discriminate on this issue, but there is an underlying reluctance, almost imperceptible, in certain private ventures where a man may be preferred to a young woman when recruiting, for fear she would keep taking leave to have babies!

SRI LANKA AT A GLANCE

'In this last Part, I purpose to speak concerning our Captivity in this Island, and during which, in what condition the English have lived there, and the eminent Providence of God in my escape thence, together with other matters relating to the Dutch and othe European Nations, that dwell and are kept there. All of which will afford so much variety and new matters, that I doubt not but the Readers will be entertained with as much delight in perusing these things, as in any else that have been already related.'
—Robert Knox

Official Name
Democratic Socialist Republic of Sri Lanka

Capital
Colombo

Flag
A lion bearing a sword in its right paw is depicted in gold on a red background with a yellow border. The lion symbolises the Sinha ancestry. Four bo leaves pointing inwards are at the four corners. They represent the four golden virtues of Buddhism: loving kindness, sympathy, joy in other's well-being and equanimity. Two vertical bands of green and orange at the mast end represent the minority ethnic groups of Muslim and Tamil.

National Anthem
Sri Lanka Matha

Time
Greenwich Mean Time + 5:30 hours (GMT + 0530)

Telephone Country Code
94

Land

Sri Lanka is an island in the Indian Ocean, just south of India

Area

Total: 65,610 sq km (25,332.2 sq miles)
Land: 64,740 sq km (24,996.3 sq miles)
Water: 870 sq km (335.9 sq miles)
Distance from north to south: 432 km (270 miles)
Distance from west to east: 224 km (140 miles)

Highest Point

Pidurutalagala (2,524 m / 8,280.8 ft)

Climate

Low Lands: tropical, minimum temperature 24.5°C (76.1°F); maximum temperature 31.7°C (89.1°F). It could get even hotter in March and April, especially in Colombo due to high humidity.

Central Hills: cooler, minimum temperature 17.1°C (62.8°F); maximum temperature 26.3°C (79.3°F). Temperatures of 4°C have been recorded in Nuwara Eliya at night.

The south-west monsoon brings rain to the western, southern and central regions from May through October, while the north-east monsoon occurs in the north and east in November through January

Population

21,324,791 (July 2009 est.)

Population by sector (2001 census)

Rural (72.2 per cent), urban (21.5 per cent), estate/plantation (6.3 per cent)

Ethnic Groups (2001 census)

Sinhalese (74.5 per cent), Sri Lankan Tamil (11.9 per cent), Sri Lankan Moors (8.3 per cent), Indian Tamil (4.6 per cent), Malays (0.3 per cent), Burghers (0.2 per cent), Others (0.2 per cent)

Religion (2001 census)
Buddhist (73.7 per cent), Hindu (11.9 per cent), Muslim (7.6 per cent), Christian (6.2 per cent), Others (0.6 per cent)

Official Languages
Sinhala and Tamil; link language: English

Government Structure
Democratic Republic with executive president and parliament; the leader of the largest parliamentary party represented in parliament is the prime minister

Administrative Divisions
Nine provinces: Central, North Central, North Western, Western, Northern, Eastern, Sabaragamuwa, Southern, Uva

Currency
Sri Lankan rupee

Gross Domestic Product (GDP)
US$ 91.9 billion (2008 est.)

Human Development Index
Rank: 99 out of 177 countries

Life Expectancy
Average: 73 years; male 71.7 years, female 77.8 years

Literacy Rate
Overall: 92.5 per cent; male 94.5 per cent; female 90.6 per cent

Natural Resources
Gems, limestone, graphite, mineral sands, phosphates, clay and hydropower

Agricultural Products
Rice, tea, rubber, coconut, sugarcane, grains, pulses, oilseed, spices; milk, eggs, hides, beef and fish

Industries

Rubber processing, tea, coconut, and other agricultural commodities; telecommunications, insurance, and banking; clothing and textiles; cement, petroleum refining and tobacco; outsourcing

Exports

Textiles and apparel; tea and spices; sapphires, cat's eye, rubies and other precious and semi-precious stones; coconut products; rubber manufactures; fish; labour—educated, skilled and unskilled

Imports

Machinery and transportation equipment, petroleum, mineral products, foodstuff, pharmaceuticals and textiles

Airports

Bandaranaike International Airport, Katunayake; Ratmalana domestic airport and Palale in Jaffna and a couple of others much smaller

ACRONYMS

Cmb	Colombo
KIA or BIA	International Airport
SLT	Sri Lanka Telecom
Rs.	Rupees

PLACES OF INTEREST

- Unesco Cultural Triangle which includes Kandy, Dambulla, Sigiriya, Anuradhapura and Polonnaruwa (tourist round ticket is available)
- Yapahuwa, Kataragama. Adam's Peak (the last during the season—December through May)
- The Dutch forts in Galle and other maritime towns, Trincomalee
- The Botanical Gardens in Peradeniya (close to Kandy) and the Hakgala Gardens (close to Nuwara Eliya)
- The Zoological Gardens in Dehiwala (suburb of Colombo) and Pinnawela elephant orphanage (on the Colombo-Kany road)

- Sinharaja forest; wild life reserves including Minneriya for elephants during July through September

FAMOUS PEOPLE
Anagarika Dharmapala (1864–1933)

Born David Hewavitharana to a wealthy business family, he was a nationalist, leader of Buddhist resurgence, founder of the Mahabodhi Society and agitated and succeeded in freeing from Hindu control the site in Buddha Gaya, which is believed to be where the Buddha attained enlightenment.

Sirimavo Ratwatte Bandaranaike (1916–2000)

The world's first woman prime minister, Sirimavo was the head of government from 1960–65 and 1970–77. She became leader of the Sri Lanka Freedom Party (SLFP) after her husband was assassinated in September 1959. She also hosted the 1976 summit of Non-Aligned Movement (NAM) in Colombo and suppressed the first uprising of Janata Vimukthi Peramuna in April 1971. She resigned as prime minister under the presidency of daughter in 2000.

Solomon West Ridgeway Dias Bandaranaike (1899–1959)

Belonged to a privileged family and husband of Sirimavo Ratwatte, he served in the State Council from 1931 and was prime minister from 1956–59. He presided over the significant shift in the country's post independence politics, making Sinhala the language of administration. He was assassinated by a Buddhist monk in 1959.

Geoffrey Bawa (1919–2003)

Sri Lanka's most distinguished and influential architect. The Parliament of Sri Lanka in Sri Jayawardene, Kotte, and Kandalama Hotel are two of his many outstanding buildings. Bawa received the Aga Khan's award for Architecture in 2001.

Radhika Coomaraswamy (1953–)

Appointed UN Special Representative for Children in Armed Conflict in March 2006. She previously held the post of UN

Special Raporteur on Violence Against Women and was the Director of the International Centre for Ethnic Studies (ICES), Colombo 7.

Gamani Corea (1925–)

Country's most distinguished economist and diplomat, who held prestigious international posts such as Secretary-General of UNCTAD (UN Conference on Trade and Development) and in NAM and SAARC, and also Chancellor of the Open University of Sri Lanka.

Rohan De Saram (1939–)

Internationally-known cellist who has performed with the major orchestras of Europe, USA and the former Soviet Union.

Junius Richard Jayawardene (1906–1996)

President of Sri Lanka from 1978–1989, he changed the constitution by modelling it on US and French constitutions, moving away from British Westminster style. He also opened the economy to market forces and resultant globalisation in 1977.

Sir William Ivor Jennings (1903–1965)

First Vice-Chancellor of the University of Ceylon and later of Peradeniya, he prepared the draft of independent Sri Lanka's constitution. He was also the Vice-Chancellor of Cambridge University from 1961–1962, and was an authority on constitutional law and author of a definitive book on the workings of the British constitution.

George Keyt (1901–1993)

Best known and most prolific of the country's modern painters, Keyt started exhibiting in the 1920s and had many solo exhibitions including ICA, London and the Art Institute, Rotterdam. He was interested in Buddhist teaching and this influence is seen in his works.

Stanley Kirinde (1928–)

A self-taught figurative painter and portraitist, Kirinde combined an active life as an artist with a full-time career in public service. He was commissioned by the Indian government to paint an official portrait of President Sri K R Narayana and his works are collected locally and internationally.

Chandrika Bandaranaike Kumaratunga (1945–)

Second daughter of Solomon West Ridgeway Dias Bandaranaike and Sirima Bandaranaike and married to Vijaya Kumaratunga, film actor turned politician (assassinated in 1988), Chandrika was president of Sri Lanka from 1994–2005.

Michael Ondaatje (1943–)

A naturalised Canadian, Ondaatje won the Booker Prize in 1992 for *The English Patient* (the film adaption earned nine Oscars). His other novels include *Anil's Ghost* and *In the Skin of a Lion*. Although he is best known as a novelist, Ondaatje's work also encompasses memoir, poetry, and film. Ondaatje placed his prize money in a trust to award the annual Gratiaen Prize for best Sri Lankan creative writing in English.

Lester James Peries (1919–) and Sumitra Peries (1935–)

Outstanding Sinhala film producers who have contributed tremendously to Sri Lankan cinematic development, including the excellent film *Rekawa*.

Velupillai Prabhakaran (1954–)

Political and military leader of the Liberation Tigers of Tamil Eelam, Prabhakaran claims to be sole representative of the Tamil people. He has carried out civil war and is guilty of having murdered Rajiv Gandhi, once prime minister of India, and several Sri Lankan leaders. Prabhakaran is wanted by Interpol's anti-terrorism branch for murder, terrorism and terrorism conspiracy. He was also sentenced in absentia for bombing the Central Bank on 31 January 1996 in Colombo, in which an estimated 90 people were killed and 1,400 injured.

Ranasinghe Premadasa (1924–1993)

Premadasa was prime minister from 1978–1989 and president of Sri Lanka from 1989–93. He introduced prioritised programmes to alleviate poverty, such as the million houses scheme and the opening of 200 garment factories in provinces to curtail unemployment. He was assassinated by the LTTE in 1993.

Barbara Sansoni (1928–)

An artist and designer of high quality cotton handloom fabrics and garments; Barbara Sansoni owns Barefoot (shop in Col 3) and is married to writer Ronald Lewcock. Her son, Dominic Sansoni, is an excellent photographer.

Don Stephen Senanayake (1884–1952)

Fondly called the 'Father of the Nation', Senanayake founded the Ceylon National Congress and the succeeding United National Party (UNP). He became the first prime minister from 1947–1952 and was later succeeded by his son Dudley Senanayake

Seneka Senanayake (1951–)

A painter with a unique style, his paintings hang in prestigious places outside and within the country.

Iranganie Serasinghe (1930–)

An outstanding actress in both English and Sinhala theatre and films. Iranganie Serasinghe is also a nature lover who established Ruk Rekaganno to protect trees and prevent deforestation in 1970.

CULTURE QUIZ

SITUATION 1

You are visiting one of the famous cultural areas of Sri Lanka. You are very impressed with a giant statue of Buddha that you see there and decide to have your photo taken with it to show to people when you get back home. As you stand there in front of the statue waiting for you friend to take the photograph, a Buddhist monk comes towards you and says something to you which you don't understand. Do you:

Ⓐ Assume that he wants to be in the photograph too and invite him to stand beside you?

Ⓑ Tell him to go away?

Ⓒ Assume that he wants a donation to the temple and give him some money?

Ⓓ Suspect that you have made a cultural error of some kind and apologise to him?

Comments

The correct answer is **D**, but what is the cultural mistake? It is considered sacrilegious in Buddhist Sri Lanka to have your photograph taken with any image of Buddha, simply because by so doing you are forced to turn your back on the image and this is never done. Similarly, you should never take a photograph of a monk—unless you have his express permission—or of a ceremony in progress, as it is presumptuous to take photographs of objects worthy of much greater respect than this. It would be equally rude to invite him to be in a photo with you (**A**), especially if you happen to be a woman, or to tell him to go away (**B**). You might offer a donation to the temple at the appropriate time (**C**) if you wish, but this would never be solicited from you by a monk at any time.

SITUATION 2

As you enter the Temple of the Tooth in Kandy, the most famous Buddhist temple in Sri Lanka, wearing your more decorous pair of shorts, a guard at the door hands you a long tubular piece of cloth, obviously expecting you to do something with you. Do you:

A Slip it around your waist and wear it like a skirt?
B Wrap it around your head?
C Assume that it is a present, thank the man and keep it?
D Try and find someone who speaks English who can tell you what to do with it?

Comments

The correct answer is **A**, because the tubular piece of cloth would be a sarong meant to cover your legs in a place of worship. Shorts should never be worn into a temple by a member of either sex, but they are particularly offensive on a woman. Some temples, like Kandy, will rent you a sarong if you are improperly dressed, but most temples will just refuse you entry if you are dressed inappropriately. **D** would probably also be an acceptable answer here, and if you were uncertain what to do, it would definitely be a better answer than **B** or **C**.

SITUATION 3

You car has broken down in a countryside road and your driver has gone off to get help. A man comes out of a nearby house and offers you some orange coloured coconuts. Do you:

A Ask him as best you can how much they cost and then bargain with him?
B Accept them as a present?
C Refuse them politely but firmly?
D Tell the man to go away and stop bothering you?

Comments

In this difficult situation, either **A** or **B** could be correct depending on the circumstance. Most Sri Lankans would assume in this situation that the man was trying to sell them the *tambili* or drinking coconut, and would also know fairly

TAKE THIS AND SHOW HIM ANSWER "A"

CULTURE SHOCK! SRI LANKA

accurately how much to offer the vendor, thus avoiding awkwardness. It is possible that the man might be offering the coconuts as a gift, for Sri Lankans are generous and have a natural inclination to help those in distress in some way. Even if you could speak no Sinhala, it would probably be apparent from the man's gestures whether he expected payment or not, and you should react accordingly. On balance, if you are in serious doubt, it is probably better to assume that they should be paid for, as the man always has the option of refusing payment when it is offered.

SITUATION 4

You have found a completely deserted beach in the south of the island, and the temptation to strip off and sunbathe in the nude is too much for you. As you lie there enjoying the sun, you hear shouts and see some villagers heading towards you. Do you:

❶ Put your clothes on hastily and run away as fast as you can?

B Put something on and then wait to greet the villagers in a friendly way?

C Shout loudly at the villagers as they approach to go away and stop invading your privacy?

D Get dressed, wait till the villagers arrive, and then apologise to them?

Comments

This is a common dilemma for some tourists—and for some villagers? By and large, nude sunbathing is not appreciated in Sri Lanka: it is, in fact, technically against the law as it offends the sensibilities of the local villagers in most places. In a situation like the one described in the question, **D** is probably the best response, though **B** would usually be quite acceptable. **C** presumes that you have a right to privacy on a Sri Lankan beach, which you do not as they are most definitely considered community property, while **A** might work—provided that you knew where you were going to run to?

SITUATION 5

While you are in Colombo, a well-dressed man approaches you on the street and tells you that he has had all his money stolen, and that he now has no bus fare to get home. He asks you to give him Rs 200 to cover the cost of the journey home. Do you:

A Give him the money as an act of charity?

B Feel fairly certain that you are being taken for a ride, but give him less than he asks just in case?

C Ignore him altogether?

D Threaten to report him to the police?

Comments

Regrettably, most people who have been in Sri Lanka for some while have a story to tell like this one. Even Sri Lankans get taken in from time to time by con artists, and there is no easy way to deal with them. Probably the best response is **C**, but this is not always easy to do, especially if the man is persistent. You can try **D**, which may have some effect, especially if you can actually see a policeman near by. **A** would be foolish as the chances of his trouble being genuine are very, very small. If you want to salve your conscience, try **B**, but it will almost certainly be a waste of your money!

SITUATION 6

You have become friendly with a Sri Lankan that you have met a few times and you ask him to drop in and visit you at home sometime when he is passing. About four weeks later, just as you are preparing to go out about 6:30 pm, your new friend arrives at your door, just 'dropping in'. Do you:

A Put off going out for half an hour or so and invite him in for a cup of tea?

B Tell him that you are terribly sorry but you are just going out now and invite him to call again sometime?

C Ask him in briefly and then a specific appointment for him to come on a pre-arranged visit?

D Take him with you where you are going?

Comments

None of these answers really solves the problem, which is the mistake that you made in the first place. Don't ask a Sri Lankan to 'drop in sometime', because if you are that vague he will take you literally, with the results described. It is much better to invite him for a specific time, to avoid any possible awkwardness and to enable both of you to make some preparations for the visit. Later, if you get to know him well, you may develop a 'dropping in' kind of friendship—which many Sri Lankans have with one another—but by then, you ought to know each other well enough that no awkwardness would develop in this situation. As far as the answers given to the actual go, **C** is probably the best of a bad lot, with only **D** being really socially unacceptable.

SITUATION 7

A raggedy old man with a cart rings your front door bell one day and points at a pile of rubbish outside on the street. Do you:

A Give him a small amount of money and gesture that he should take it away?

HOW MUCH TO REMOVE IT OR HOW MUCH TO CLIMB IT AND PLANT A FLAG ON TOP?

❸ Tell him to go away?

❹ Have your servant tell him to go away?

❺ Ask your servant to tell him that he should clear the rubbish away regularly and that he will be paid for his services at the end of the year?

Comments

There are a number of people on the streets of major Sri Lankan cities who are looking for ways of earning a little money. Municipal garbage services do exist, and will remove your basic household rubbish twice or thrice a week as a matter of course. Other refuse such as garden debris and a broken item is usually not removed in the regular clearance and it may be necessary to pay someone to take it away. ❹ would therefore be appropriate in some circumstances, particularly if the rubbish had been left there for some time. You could try ❺ if you have occasion to dispose of unusual items on a regular basis. ❸ and ❹ are both possible depending on the circumstances and the degree of persistence used by the caller.

SITUATION 8

You servant tells you one morning that his cousin-brother is sick in the country and that he must go away for a few days to see what has to be done. Do you

❹ Refuse permission on the grounds that there ought to be someone closer who could look after the sick person?

❸ Tell him that he can go but that you will dock his wages for each day that he is away?

❺ Assume that he is lying because this relationship doesn't exist and that he is only trying to get a few extra days off?

❻ Allow him to go?

Comments

Strange as it may seem, ❻ is the only possible answer here. Looking after a relative is one of the duties that most Sri Lankans feel strongly about, and it is not uncommon to go

some distance to help out if asked. Employers know this and are usually quite willing to grant time off for this purpose, without strings attached, providing that it can be conveniently arranged. **Ⓐ** would betray severe cultural insensitivity, while **Ⓑ** would be considered mean. If **Ⓒ** was your answer, you had better look for a new servant as you obviously don't' have much trust in this one!

SITUATION 9

You are planning a dinner party to which you have invited both a Hindu and a Muslim as well as other guests. You are having trouble coming up with a suitable menu. Do you:

Ⓐ Serve what you would serve at a normal Western dinner party without any special concessions?

Ⓑ Decide to serve no pork or beef dishes at all?

Ⓒ Serve a vegetable meal to be on the safe side?

Ⓓ Serve a normal meal, but indicate clearly in some way the dishes that contain pork and beef?

Comments

This is a dilemma often faced by those who have to entertain officially abroad, and there is no clear solution. **Ⓑ** is safest, as

serving fish or chicken will raise no religious or social hackles. **D** would be acceptable at a buffet dinner or cocktail party but not at a sit-down affair. **C** restricts choices unnecessarily, though it is sometimes an option for change, while **A** is a recipe for potential disaster!

SITUATION 10

An employee misses a day's work with no explanation, and when he turns up for work the next day, offers only the vague excuse that he had pressing matters to attend to which meant he couldn't come to work on that day. Do you:

A Tell him that he will lose a day's pay?

B Insist that he tell you the exact reason that he was away and then punish him?

C Accept his explanation but remind him that he must try and let you know if he cannot come into work?

D Tell that this is inexcusable and that if it happens again you will dismiss him?

Comments

There is no correct answer here. **A** would be a possibility if the employee could not come up with any answer that is

satisfactory, but would probably be extreme in most cases. **B** and **D** would show that you are probably not a very good manager in any case, as you lack both cultural and personal sensitivity to others, while **C** is probably the best option in most situations. Of course, the actual answer would depend on both the employee and the reason that he eventually gave, but this is not as uncommon situation in Sri Lanka due to the lack of universal communication, and is usually dealt with in a fairly lenient manner.

DO'S AND DON'TS

There are many possible suggestions in Sri Lanka for things to do and situations to be avoided. The following are some of the most important:

DO'S
- Leave your preconceptions about the country behind when you come.
- Reciprocate friendly overtures.
- Observe dress requirements when visiting places of worship.
- Try the local food.
- Try wearing a sarong or a *sari*.

DON'TS
- Don't judge Sri Lanka on first impressions.
- Don't serve pork to Muslims or beef to Hindus.
- Don't drink the water without boiling it first.
- Don't let the presence of persistent beggars irritate you.
- Don't create offence by ignoring cultural norms.

Sensitivity, common sense and a little local knowledge form the basis for judgement of how to behave appropriately in Sri Lanka. Using these, it is fairly difficult to put a foot seriously wrong.

GLOSSARY

A SURVIVAL GUIDE TO SINHALA AND TAMIL

English	Sinhala	Tamil
Welcome	Ayubowan	Vanakkam
How are you?	Kohomada?	Eppady Sugam?
Goodbye	Ayubowan	Vanakkam
Thanks	Istuty	Nanry
Where are you going?	Koheda yanne?	Enga poreenga?
What is your name?	Nama mokakda?	Ungada peyar enna?
How many are in the family?	Pavule keedenek innavada?	Ungada kudumbathi ethanai per?
Are you married?	Oba kasada bendalada?	Neenga thirumanam anavara?
Are you working?	Oba rassawak karanawada?	Neenga velai seihireengala?
Where are you working?	Oba koheda weda karanne?	Neenga engay velai seihireenga?
This place is beautiful	Methana lassanai	Intha idam alahana irukkirathu
This food is very tasty	Me kema hari rasai	Inda sappadu nalla rusi
I will come tomorrow	Mama heta enava	Naan nalai varen
I am not feeling well	Mata saneepa nehe	Enakku sugam illai
I don't understand	Mata therenne nehe	Enakku vilanga illai

SRI LANKAN RELATIONSHIPS

English	Sinhala	Kandyan Sinhala (if different)
mother	*amma*	
father	*thaththa*	*appachchi*
grandmother	*aachi*	*athamma*
grandfather	*seeya*	*atha*
maternal-aunt (older to mother)	*loku amma*	
maternal-aunt (younger)	*punchi amma*	*kuda amma*
paternal-aunt	*nanda*	*nandamma*
maternal-uncle	*mama*	
paternal-uncle (older to father)	*loku thaththa*	*loku appachchi*
paternal-uncle (younger)	*bappa*	*cuda appachchi*
older sister	*akka*	
younger sister	*nangi*	
older brother	*aiya*	
younger brother	*malli*	
daughter	*duwa*	
son	*putha*	
sister-in-law	*nana*	
brother-in-law	*massina*	
daughter-in-law	*leli*	
son-in-law	*bena*	
mother-in-law	*nandamma*	
father-in-law	*mamandi*	

No term exists for cousins. All cousins are referred to with the same term as for brother and sister.

RESOURCE GUIDE

COMMUNICATIONS

Sri Lanka has a well-developed communication system, and both internal and external communication is efficient. Most of the major hotels offer such services as international direct dialling, telex, fax and email, and there are also a number of bureaus dotted about the city of Colombo which offer the same services for a fee. Telephoning within the country is also efficient since direct dialling is possible.

The postal service is quite efficient, and letters posted in Colombo usually reach their destinations speedily. When posting letters to countries outside Sri Lanka which require high denomination stamps, make sure that you have them franked in the post office where you buy them to ensure that they remain on the letters! Try and avoid using post boxes if you can as well: not all of them are emptied on the most regular basis and you might just pick one that has not yet received its annual visitation!

EMBASSIES AND HIGH COMMISSION

The SLT Rainbow Pages volume of the Sri Lanka Telecom National Telephone Directory lists 113 countries represented by embassies, high commissions and consulates, very few of which are situated in New Delhi, India. Addresses, telephone, telex, fax numbers and email addresses are included in most entries. India, France, the UK and US have detailed entries giving names and residence telephone numbers of diplomatic staff, and organisations attached to them. Embassies or high commissions in Sri Lanka, and their consular divisions, can assist their nationals in an emergency. Don't forget, however, that most embassies and high commissions cannot help you if you have broken Sri Lankan law, and can only assist in helping you within the limits of what is allowed to anyone accused of a crime.

Other foreign representations such as the UN, ICRC and Asian Development Bank, to name but three of the 23 listed, are also included with the necessary data.

EMERGENCIES

In an emergency, your hotel or embassy should be able to provide you with a list of whom to contact. If it is an emergency that needs instant attention, one of the following numbers listed in the SLT National Telephone Directory would prove useful, depending on the nature of the emergency.

- Fire   242-2222
- Police   119
- Police (Colombo)   243-3333
- Bomb disposal   243-4215
- Accident service   269-1111

FINDING YOUR WAY AROUND

Contrary to what you might expect, maps of Sri Lanka are quite easy to find and surprisingly good. The two most popular are called *The Tourist Map of Sri Lanka* and *A Tourist Map of Colombo*, both of which are comprehensive and easily obtainable at hotels and bookshops. If you need something more comprehensive, the survey department of the government maintains a retail outlet in Fort just opposite the Hilton Hotel, and small-scale survey maps of all parts of the country can be bought here. You can also buy reproductions of old maps of Sri Lanka here, and they are good value as souvenirs.

Navigating your way around Sri Lanka using a map is not hard, as most of the major towns are signposted and the place names quite logical—and rather fun to interpret. Most are listed in the three languages: Sinhala, Tamil and English. At first, a number of Sri Lankan town names seem very long, but they are nearly always compounds and if you remember a few simple rules, you should be able to handle the long names like a native! Here are a few hints:

duwa	island
gama	village
ganga	river
mawatha	street

nuwara	city
oya	stream
pura	town
tota	port
vihara	temple
wewa	lake

HEALTH

With a minimum number of sensible precautions, your health should not be a problem in Sri Lanka. There is considerable debate about whether to take anti-malarial tablets in Sri Lanka or not, and you will get conflicting advice about this. In Colombo, it is not usually necessary, though if you are going to be out of Colombo for an extended period, it might be a wise precaution. It is better to prevent mosquito bites as far as possible by rubbing repellent creams on you, sleeping in air-conditioned rooms or under a net with a fan going full blast. The dengue mosquito is a morning creature, so beware before noon! Water-borne diseases are not common if you are careful, nor should you get any form of food poisoning. Lomotil is a useful drug to carry around with you if you are prone to diarrhoea, but should be used sparingly and only when needed. A basic first aid kit of other drugs is also something useful to have in your possession, as medical services outside Colombo are sometimes fairly rudimentary.

TOURIST INFORMATION

Sri Lanka is very well aware of the need to attract tourists to the island and to counter the negative publicity which the country received by LTTE propagandists, and hence tourists are assiduously looked after. There are a number of companies who provide services for the tourist, noticeably in the car hire business, and any of the major companies listed in the phone book will set up an itinerary for you to go around the island in a chauffeur-driven car at modest cost.

Exploitation of the tourist does exist in Sri Lanka, but it is not common and usually easily avoided by sticking to the reputable companies who have been dealing for some time with the needs of tourists. Hotel staff are more often than not extremely polite, and give the visitor a taste of Sri Lankan hospitality!

FURTHER READING

This bibliography is divided into sections, each of which focuses on a different area. It is impossible to include all the books written on every aspect of Sri Lanka, as Sri Lankans are fairly prolific in their writing in English, and there are many such books. We have tried to select the best—or at least the most informative—for those who want to know more about some of the topics discussed in the pages of this book.

GUIDE BOOKS/TOURIST INFORMATION
(Folders, brochures on places, beaches, flora and fauna are available free on request from the Ceylon Tourist Board, Galle Road, Colombo 3.)

Accommodation Guide. Colombo: Ceylon Tourist Board.

Lonely Planet Sri Lanka (the latest edition). Richard Plunkett and Brigitte Ellemor. Victoria: Lonely Planet Publications.

Official Handbook of Sri Lanka (in English, French and German). Colombo: Ceylon Tourist Board, quarterly.

Gateway to Kandy, Ancient Monuments in the Central Hills of Sri Lanka. Anuradha Senewiratne. Colombo: Vijitha Yapa, 2008.

Insight Guide—Sri Lanka (Discovery Channel). London: APA publications (latest).

Rhythm of Cascades: 100 waterfalls: a photographic window of selected waterfalls in Sri Lanka. M S N L de Costa Colombo: Printcare, 2007.

Sri Lanka, the Resplendent Isle. Dominic Sansoni and Richard Simon. Singapore: Times Editions Pte Ltd, 1989.

The Diversity of Sri Lankan Wildlife by Jayantha Jayawardene. Colombo: (Author), 2008.

This Month in Sri Lanka. Colombo: Spectrum Lanka Ltd, monthly.

Travel Lanka: Comprehensive monthly guide to travellers in Sri Lanka. ISSN 1800-1149

SPECIFIC TOPICS
Caste in Modern Ceylon: The Sinhala System in Transition. Ryan Bryce. New Jersey: Rutgers University Press, 1953.

Sigiriya: City, Palace and Royal Gardens. Seneka Senanayake. Colombo: Central Cultural Fund, Ministry of Cultural Affairs, 1999.

Vanished Trails: The Last of the Veddhas. Richard Lionel Spittel. Colombo: The Associated Newspapers of Ceylon, 1961.

Veddhas in Transition. Nandadeva Wijesekera. Colombo: M D Gunasena, 1964.

Biography
Personalities of Sri Lanka: A Biographical Study (15th–20th century) 1490–1990 AD. Dr K D G Wimalaratne. Colombo: Ceylon Business Appliances Ltd, 1994.

Ceremonies/Festivals
The Kandy Esala Perahera—Asia's Most Spectacular Pageant. M B Dasanayake. Colombo: Ranco Publishers, 1977.

Manners, Customs and Ceremonies of Sri Lanka. Miniwan P Tillakaratne. New Delhi: Sri Satgura Publishers, 1986.

Cookery
Ceylon Cookery. Chandra Dissanayake. Colombo: Metro Printers, 1976.

Ceylon Daily News Cookery Book. Hilda Deutrom. Colombo: Associated Newspaper of Ceylon, 1964.

Encyclopedia
Encyclopedia of Sri Lanka. C A Gunawardene. New Delhi: Sterling Pub Ltd, 2003.

Ethnic Conflict
Political Violence in Sri Lanka 1971–1987. Gamini Samranayake. New Delhi: Gyan Pub. House, 2008.

Reaping the Whirlwind: Ethnic Conflict, Ethnic Politics in Sri Lanka. K M De Silva. New Delhi: Penguin Books, 1998.

Sri Lanka's Ethnic Crisis & National Security. Rohan Gunaratna. Colombo: South Asian Network on Conflict Research, 1998.

The Other Lanka. Hongkong: Asian Human Rights Commission (AHRC), 2006.

Tortured Island and the Price of Peace. Malinga H Gunaratne. Ratmalana: Vishva Lekha, 2005

Heritage
BAWA: Geoffrey Bawa: the complete worlds. David Robson. London: Thames and Hudson, 2002.

Heritage of Sri Lanka. Pundit Dr Nandedeva Wijesekera. Colombo: Archaeological Society of Sri Lanka, 1984.

Viharas and Verandahs. Barbara Sansoni. Colombo: Ranco Publishers, 1980.

History
A History of Sri Lanka. K M De Silva. Colombo: Vijitha Yapa Pub, 2005.

Language
A Dictionary of Sri Lankan English. Michael Meyler. Colombo: (Author), 2007.

Say It in Sinhala. J B Dissanayake. Colombo: Lake House Investments, 1993.

Tamil. K Kailasapathy. Colombo: Department of Cultural Affairs, 1976.

Sinhala Phrase Book (2nd edition). Swarna Pragnaratne. Victoria: Lonely Planet Publications, 2002.

Mythology/Folklore
Myths of the Hindus and Buddhists. Ananda K Coomaraswamy and Sister Nivedita. London: Kessinger Publishing, 2003.

Sinhalese Folklore, Folk Religion and Folk Life. Nandasena Ratnapala. Colombo: Sarvodaya Research Institute, 1980.

Sri Lanka's Mythology. K Weerakoon. Colombo: Samayawadhana, 1985.

Sri Lankan Folk Tales for Suren and Amrit. Nanda P Wanasundera. Ratmalana: Vishva Lekha, 2006.

Religion
A Short History of Hinduism in Ceylon and Three Essays on the Tamils. C S Navaratnam, 1964.

Origin and Development of the Hindu Religion and People. C Sivaratnam. Colombo: Ranco Publishers, 1980.

The Seven Stages of Purification and the Insight Knowledges. Ven Matara Sri Nanarama. Kandy: Buddhist Publications Society, 1983.

What the Buddha Taught. Walpola Rahula. Oxford, UK: Oneworld Publications Ltd, 1997.

SRI LANKAN LIFE (ANNOTATED)
The Winds of Sinhala. Colin de Silva. London: HarperCollins Publishers, 1983.

The Founts of Sinhala. Colin de Silva. London: HarperCollins Publishers, 1985.

The Fires of Sinhala. Colin de Silva. London: HarperCollins Publishers, 1987.

- An absorbing trilogy about the historical founding of Sri Lanka, using historical characters in fictionalised situations. Very good source of information about the origins of many aspects of current Sri Lanka.

An Historical Relation of Ceylon. Robert Knox. New Delhi: Navrang, 2004.

- A detailed description of the Kandyan kingdom, the king and people.

Running in the Family. Michael Ondaatje. London: Vintage Press, 1993.

- An absorbing autobiographical journey of discovery by an expatriate Sri Lankan poet, novelist and Booker Prize winner, who returned to the country to find his roots. Some brilliant and sympathetic insights into the life of the Burgher people.

Savage Sanctuary. Richard L Spittel. Colombo: Colombo Book Centre, 1953.

- A novel about the Veddhas, written from the personal experience of someone who lived with them and who has written extensively about their lifestyle.

The Sweet and Simple Kind. Yasmine Gooneratne. Colombo: Perera and Hussein, 2006.

- A fictionalised novel of a politicised family in the 1950s and 60s. Short-listed for the Commonwealth Writers Prize 2007.

The Village in the Jungle. Leonard Woolf. London: Eland, 2006.

- Written after a term of office in the Ceylon Civil Service in the first decade of the century, and still considered to be the best novel in English about Sri Lanka.

ABOUT THE AUTHORS

Robert Barlas was born in England, but has always had the wanderlust in his veins. At the age of 19, he migrated to Canada, which has been his home—on and off—for the last 25 years.

A retired teacher, Bob has made a career out of working in international education all over the world, concentrating mainly in Asia. Among the countries he has worked in are England, New Zealand, Singapore, the People's Republic of China and Sri Lanka. Bob and his family had lived in Colombo where both he and his wife, Nancy, taught at the Overseas Children's School, which his two children, Richard and Sharine, attended as students. The family travelled all over Sri Lanka—even into parts of the country which were nominally off limits to foreigners—and made a large number of Sri Lankan friends. The Barlases left Sri Lanka in 1989 and returned to their home in Canada, at least until their wanderlust takes them overseas again!

Bob enjoys reading, writing, skiing and sailing, and, of course, travelling, which has taken him and most of his family to over 80 countries so far—the rest of the world he is still working on!

Nanda Pethiyagoda Wanasundera, the youngest in a family of six, was born in her mother's ancestral home in a village near Kandy, in central Sri Lanka. She had a conservative upbringing until she broke away from the sheltered life of home and boarding school to enter teacher training collage. She married Suriya Wanasundera, hers being a love marriage, unlike her siblings', all of whom consented to proposed matches. After 20 years of teaching, she obtained professional qualifications and shifted to librarianship. She has two sons, one in business management and the other an architect. She is now a grandmother of two boys.

The abiding passion in her life is her love for her country. Her maternal grandfather sowed the seeds of this love in her by taking her on pilgrimage to Anuradhapura and Polonnaruwa. Her father often took the family on journeys across the country. He died when she was six. Her brothers and sisters continued the trend. Her husband, a thrice-a-year-vacationer would select out of the way places where they would stay in rented circuit bungalows and cut themselves off from city life. Widowed, she leads a quieter life now, her two sons working and living abroad.

Her main interests are meeting people, going to the cinema and theatre (both limited in Sri Lanka), and reading about them in international newspapers and journals. A freelance journalist, she has a column in a Sunday newspaper and reviews books and films. She has six published books to her credit. She is a practicing Buddhist and strives to accept the good and the unsatisfactory in her life and in her country, with equanimity.

204

INDEX

Titles in the CultureShock! series:

Argentina	Hawaii	Sri Lanka
Australia	Hong Kong	Shanghai
Austria	Hungary	Singapore
Bahrain	India	South Africa
Beijing	Ireland	Spain
Belgium	Italy	Sri Lanka
Berlin	Jakarta	Sweden
Bolivia	Japan	Switzerland
Borneo	Korea	Syria
Bulgaria	Laos	Taiwan
Brazil	London	Thailand
Cambodia	Malaysia	Tokyo
Canada	Mauritius	Travel Safe
Chicago	Morocco	Turkey
Chile	Munich	United Arab
China	Myanmar	Emirates
Costa Rica	Netherlands	USA
Cuba	New Zealand	Vancouver
Czech Republic	Norway	Venezuela
Denmark	Pakistan	
Ecuador	Paris	
Egypt	Philippines	
Finland	Portugal	
France	Russia	
Germany	San Francisco	
Great Britain	Saudi Arabia	
Greece	Scotland	

For more information about any of these titles, please contact any of our Marshall Cavendish offices around the world (listed on page ii) or visit our website at:

www.marshallcavendish.com/genref